PORTRAIT OF THE COTSWOLDS

THE PORTRAIT SERIES

Portrait of
THE COTSWOLDS

EDITH BRILL

LONDON
ROBERT HALE & COMPANY

© Edith Brill 1964, 1968 and 1971
First published in Great Britain 1964
Reprinted 1964
Second edition February 1968
Third edition December 1971
Reprinted January 1973

Robert Hale & Company
63 Old Brompton Road
London, S.W.7

ISBN 0 7091 2498 8

PRINTED IN GREAT BRITAIN BY
LOWE AND BRYDONE (PRINTERS) LTD., THETFORD, NORFOLK

CONTENTS

ILLUSTRATIONS

ACKNOWLEDGEMENTS

Nos. 7, 12 (bottom), 14 and 19 are reproduced from photographs by Geoffrey N. Wright; the remainder were supplied by Eagle Photos, Cheltenham.

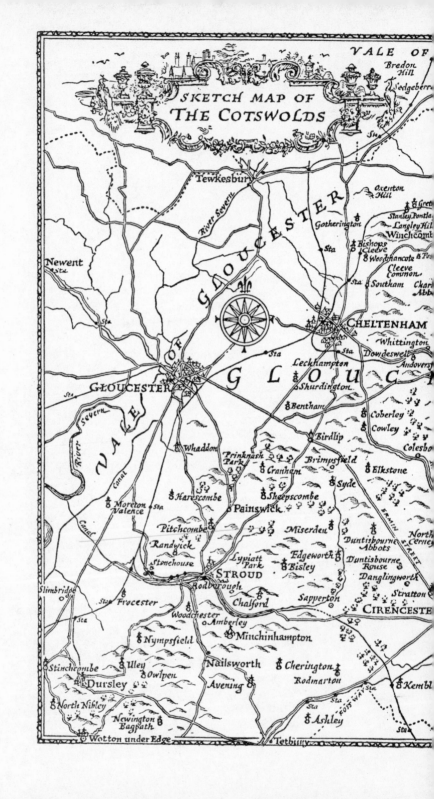

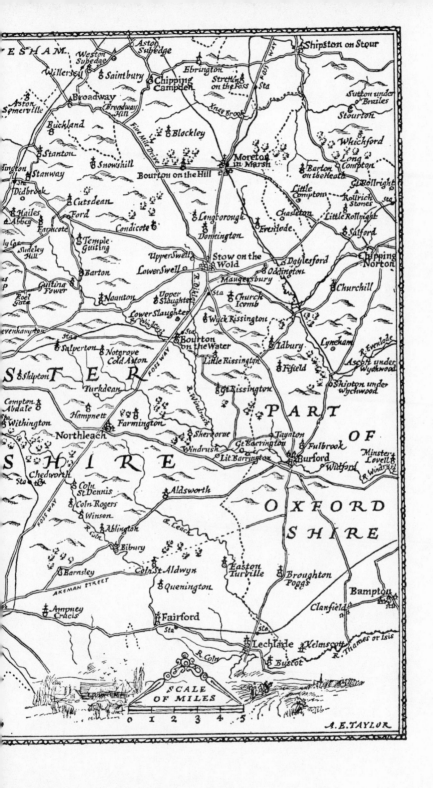

It cannot but give us cause to wonder, and to say, out of our old forefather's fields, We reape the best fruites of our modern understanding.

John Smythe, 1601

COTSWOLD STONE

A PORTRAIT of a region, like the portrait of a person, depends on the hard structure beneath the surface; the bones are a more essential part of its make-up than the flesh. The bony structure of the Cotswolds is oolitic limestone or roe-stone, a rock composed of small rounded granules of calcium carbonate pressed tightly together like the roe of a fish. The word "oolite" comes from two Greek words meaning "egg" and "stone" and to identify it no other description than its name is necessary.

There are two kinds of oolite, the Inferior Oolite, an older and lower stratum of this limestone, and the Great Oolite, a newer rock in the geological tables whose grains are slightly smaller. When newly dug it varies in colour from bright orange buff to pale cream according to the depth and location of the quarries. The Inferior floors the larger part of the region, tilting upwards at its western edge and including the highest reaches of the wolds. In the south Cotswolds the belt is much smaller and is soon followed behind the escarpment by the Great Oolite, which also follows eastwards in the other part of the region extending into and across Oxfordshire.

Although every countryside must be conditioned to some extent by its basic rocks this is not always obvious to the eye, but on the Cotswolds it is impossible not to be aware of limestone most of the time. The stone provides the material, beneath ground and above it, worked and unworked, which gives the Cotswolds their unique distinction. The comparative softness of the rock is responsible for the formation of the wolds into smoothly moulded undulations without harsh contours or angularities. In the north the hills have such a wide sweep and amplitude that the eye ranges far before a curve is completed and another begins. In the south the folds of the hills are more intricate, the valleys more ravine-like, but the landscape still keeps its gracious, sweetly-flowing lines in true affinity with the arc of the skies above them.

The vegetation derives a special quality from the limestone soil as well as from the altitude. Planted avenues, groves, clumps and hanging woods of beech are part of the characteristic upland scene, accentuating the contours where they stand out on a sky-line or clothe a hillside. The wild flowers and grasses quicken a botanist's pulse because this is the habitat of many rare and beautiful lime-loving plants, while the more common ones grow boun-teously along the waysides and on slopes too steep to plough.

Vast arable fields have now taken the place of the open sheep-walks of earlier days, and from early summer to harvest they are seas of rippling green, bronze and gold, reacting to every change of light, every movement of the wind; and there are few days on Cotswold when the wind is quiet. Barley, particularly, is a crop which thrives well on the well-drained shallow soil. I have seen it looking superb in dry summers when cracks have appeared in the parched ground a foot or more deep. In some of the fields one has only to scratch the ground to find stone, and after ploughing many an upland field is so covered with stone brash one might easily mistake it for a surface quarry.

Cobbett commented on this during one of his Rural Rides in 1826. "The soil is what is called a Stone Brash below, with a reddish earth mixed with little bits of this brash at top, and, for the greater part of the wold, even this soil is very shallow." Great progress has been made since his day in the development of types of corn suitable for the region, and if Cobbett could see the great fields of wheat, oats and barley grown today they would delight his heart. Later on in the same Ride he admits rather grudgingly that he saw "in some places, decent crops" and "some of the finest ox-teams that I ever saw".

Sidney Smith, like Cobbett, did not care for Cotswold country, calling it a region of "stone and sorrow". He may have had reasons for the word "sorrow", but I suspect the way it tripped off the tongue prompted its use.

What they both felt and what is very true is that there is nothing cosy about the wolds. The most ardent lover will admit that seen under a low cloud-packed sky, in the north of the region particularly, they can appear bleak and austere: for those with a feeling for the bare bones of a landscape this austerity is part of its fascination. The scene often seems more remote from civilization than the mileage shown on the map. One of the pleasures of walking on the hills is this sense of being alone in a region which is never many miles from a busy main road.

When man wanted to build on Cotswold the stone was under his feet. Some beds of oolite give a fine-grained stone called freestone, easily cut and sawn into blocks when newly quarried but hardening on exposure. This freestone provided the main fabric of his building. The roofing tiles came from a special kind of surface quarry, the stone being dug in the autumn and left exposed all the winter. It then splits easily along the joints where thin films of clay have frozen and expanded. As well as these frosted tiles there are others which occur naturally and are called, with the worker's instinct for the expressive word, "presents". Presents are found in thin-layered rock and are easily quarried in thicknesses almost ready for use.

The history of stone-roofing is a fascinating one, for down the ages the tiler has invented names for the various sizes and thicknesses as well as for the special tools he uses for laying them. The names differ from district to district, emphasizing something we rarely remember in these days of easy transport, the difficulty of carrying building material in hill country before motor-lorries were common and when villages and towns only a few miles distant were cut off from one another because of the natural barriers made by the steep hill roads.

As well as providing the material for churches, manor-houses, farms and cottages the stone was used for the smaller necessities of rural life, those things usually made of timber in lowland districts. The scarcity of timber on the bare uplands was not a problem when stone for gateposts, stiles, troughs and corn-bins, for walling fields, orchards and gardens, was close at hand to be had for the digging.

The earliest buildings in Cotswold stone left to us today are the long barrows of the New Stone Age, placed where they commanded the widest views if not actually on the highest points of the hills. Their chambers and roofs are made of blocks of stone, often with dry-walling sealing the passages and finishing off the tombs. Walling such as that found at Belas Knap, the famous long barrow above Winchcombe, shows how well these ancient builders knew their job. The stones have a thinness and regularity of shape rarely excelled by later wallers. The Ministry of Works has reconstructed the horned entrance using new stone slates to supplement the old, for many were lost and spoilt when the barrow lay denuded and broken after the excavations of 1863. It is possible to pick out the old stones from the new by their dark grey colour, though the new ones are now weathering beautifully to a soft grey. I never look at them without a sense of wonder that the craft should have lasted unchanged for four thousand years.

Stone walling no longer employs many workers regularly today, wire fencing being quicker and cheaper to erect. I doubt if it is as durable, for a well laid dry-stone wall with the stones properly interlocking is not easily broken down and unlike wire fencing grows more comely with age. One can still see lengths of old wall skilfully repaired, though nowadays the "toppers" or "combers" finishing it off are often laid in cement. This may offend some traditionalists but where a road flanks a public highway it keeps irresponsible vandals from pushing the "toppers" off.

Not so many months ago I watched an elderly man near Cirencester restoring a wall which had fallen into decay. To begin with he had to dismantle the ruins and he did this with considerable care, scrutinizing each stone before putting it aside in one of the several heaps beside him.

"Wouldn't it be quicker to push it down?" I asked, hoping to provoke him into talking to me, for when I had wished him "Good Morning" his taciturn reply had told me he was not the kind of man who talked easily to strangers.

He straightened his back, frowning as if considering whether he should give my remark serious attention. When he decided I was not just making conversation his long thin face creased into a rather stony smile and he began to talk about his work like an enthusiast. As I listened my pleasure was divided between the way his bright blue eyes lit up when he was animated, his voice native as the stone he handled, and the things he told me. Without a battering ram, he explained, it would be difficult to demolish the wall, illustrating the point by giving it a vigorous push. When the dust had cleared I could see that only a small v-shaped portion had tumbled to the ground.

He went on to say that it was quicker and more economical in the long run to take off a few stones at a time. By handling them he could put aside those fit to be used in the rebuilding and throw away the rubbish. He showed me how the stones interlocked and overlapped each other and how at intervals larger stones helped to keep the smaller ones firm and tight, and how the wall was laid on a foundation of larger squarish blocks a few inches below the level of the ground.

Choosing the right stones was the important thing, he said, speaking freely now but with deliberation to emphasize each point.

"How do you know the right kind of stone to use?" I asked.

Walling stone, it seems, must come from a certain kind of quarry and have been dug at the right time of year, otherwise frost would crumble and split it and ruin the wall in its first winter. When I asked him to be more explicit he shook his head. "I just know. With handling it," he said.

Once upon a time, for walling had had its golden age in his father's time, the quarryman would select stone for the job, but today they sent him "any old rough" so that he had to shape most pieces with his hammer. "Like the coal we get. Too much rubbish and not enough good stuff," he added dryly.

He showed me his fingers roughened and sore because of the sharp edges of the shells in the stone. "They're worse in wet weather, but bad enough in the dry. It's the lime dust, dries up the sap. I had a young man once wanting to learn walling, but he soon gave up because his fingers got so sore he couldn't play his gittar, and that mattered more to him than his work, I reckon."

He took some fossils out of his pocket. "Sea-shells. I knocks them out for the schoolmaster. He says all this as far as Birdlip was once under the sea."

Giving me a rather sheepish look as if he were a little ashamed of talking about such things he put the fossils away, but I could see the wonder of it appealed to him. A long line of army trucks and gun carriers passed us shattering the pleasant quietness of the road. I was tempted to quote to him two lines of poetry which often come to mind when I see fossils in Cotswold stone:

> There, where the long street roars, hath been
> The stillness of the central sea,

but instead I thanked him warmly for his help and went on my way.

Cotswold possesses a small architectural world of its own. Though it only covers part of the great belt of oolitic limestone running across England from Dorset to Lincolnshire, where the chief building material from the thirteenth century to the nineteenth was stone dug from local quarries and where the same style of architecture prevailed, this style is less diluted and reaches its greatest perfection within the Cotswold area. It also acquired its own name, "the Cotswold vernacular", because of the necessity to define it.

The main part of the Cotswolds is in Gloucestershire, but outliers and offshoots spill over into Somerset, Worcestershire, Warwickshire, Oxfordshire and Wiltshire. It is not possible to give the boundaries of the region to within a few miles. Those who live on the borderland or near borderland insist upon being taken in, and there are a few places nearer the centre not worthy of the name. By beginning roughly at the south-west escarpment above Bath, with Fairford and Burford bordering the south-east and Chipping Campden and Meon Hill making its northern limits I am not saying Cotswold begins or ends at any of these places. Each lover of the region has his own views on the subject and knowing the passion this can arouse I am willing to acquiesce with all.

During its most productive years, from the late sixteenth century to the beginning of the eighteenth century, when the wool and clothing trades flourished, the manor-houses, farms and cottages achieved their greatest comeliness, and it is the buildings erected within this period, restored and modernized, which give the villages and little towns their unique distinction today. The most familiar features are dormer windows, gables, steep-pitched roofs covered with stone slates, Tudor windows with transoms, mullions and drip mouldings; in short an Elizabethan style which continued long after the Elizabethan period because it was admirably suited to the building material and local conditions.

The dormer window evolved because of the lack of height of the walls. Cottage walls rarely rose above sixteen feet from ground to eaves; the average height is fifteen and many are not higher than fourteen. Owing to the steep-pitched roof this left

Cotswold gables, Painswick

only about five feet above the level of the upper floor, leaving no room for windows under the eaves. By carrying the walls into miniature gables windows could be inserted, thus forming the dormer.

In the more important and larger houses dormers could be finished with carved copings, finials or stone-slate verges according to the mason's taste or the taste of his customers, producing a variety of treatment and ornament never out of keeping with the simplicity of the main design and accentuating it. It is these adornments which add charm and individuality to the buildings. As a contrast the massive simplicity of the stone chimney stacks with or without mouldings in their two or three stages produce a sense of balance and sturdiness, rooting the buildings, as it were, firmly to the ground. One of the most attractive features of the seventeenth-century house is the chamber gable and, in some instances, a pair of such gables linked by a porch.

The pattern of the English village as we knew it until the changes of the last two decades consisted of three main classes of domestic buildings, the cottage of the farm worker, a few middle class homes and the manor-house or mansion of the squire. The cottages of rough stone and rubble were erected, or in many instances thrown together, without any architectural pretensions, often by the cottagers themselves with the aid of a mason, their function being to provide a hearth for cooking and warmth and shelter when the day's work was over. The better kind of house was raised by semi-skilled craftsmen, mostly mobile workers relying on more highly trained men for the masonry dressings. The manor-house of good freestone was built by masons according to the taste and means of the owner.

The Dissolution of the monasteries freed large numbers of masons who had been permanently attached to these establishments, and Gloucestershire was rich in religious houses as the old saying "As sure as God's in Gloucestershire" proves. Many of these men and their descendants turned to domestic building as well as work on parish churches, travelling from one village to another wherever employment was to be found. It is to these stone masons we owe much of the good building in Cotswold villages, not only for the fabric of houses which have survived for three hundred years or more but for the small adorning graces.

2

A South Cotswold landscape

The skill learned and practised on the decorative details of monasteries and abbeys thus came to be adapted for less inspired work; it is easy to imagine that some of the finials and small carvings finishing off secular buildings were produced because the craftsmen could not resist the pleasure of using their carving tools as well as their trowels.

By the eighteenth century Renaissance influence began to percolate slowly into the countryside. It was probably introduced by those wealthy merchants and landed gentry whose business and pleasure made them familiar with the new styles of architecture coming into fashion in London and other big cities. First becoming evident in the rebuilding of old manor-houses in new parkland it reached the villages and little towns in the beginning as additions and alterations to older houses, to give them the new look by means of porches, doorways and sash windows. The weathering qualities of local stone subdued the Classic style and it now appears as natural a part of the scene as the native gothic. One reason why these eighteenth-century houses are not out of place in a Cotswold village street is that they are seldom large enough to dominate the general picture; a touch of eighteenth-century urbanity providing contrast as well as a sense of continuity.

The same century also saw the beginning of village housing as a single unit, for this was the period when landscape planning was considered a landowner's duty. Where a village belonged to a family interested in improving their estate and the living conditions of their workers the old cottages were pulled down and others of a neater appearance built in their place. Sherborne, near Northleach, is a good example of this kind of village.

The new cottages were designed as picturesque appendages to the Big House. In those days the landowners had not heard of the Cotswold vernacular and followed their own fancies or those of their womenfolk or agents. George Eliot's *Middlemarch* gives an interesting picture of the attitude of country squires to their labourers' housing. As they were generally all of the same pattern the intentional quaintness could look monotonous and I fancy that living in these somewhat regimented dwellings also helped to subdue their occupants to a general pattern of behaviour, keeping them within the close confines of their own class system.

When in my younger days, long before every cottage had radio and television and was occupied by retired gentlefolk, we went exploring the Cotswolds we soon learnt to avoid this kind of village, finding it suspicious if not actually hostile to strangers, the cottagers unwilling to talk freely to us, probably because we did not fit into any social group they recognized. We were looking for the last vestiges of folklore and did not want to enlist the help of the local parson or schoolmistress, having found this defeated our purpose of getting the villagers to talk naturally. Most of this form of feudalism has now disappeared, and it is ironic that the villages where it still lingers in spirit if not in reality are amongst the most attractive today.

In the villages where the squalid and the picturesque existed side by side and often intermingled we were accepted with the tolerance of your true countryman always ready to be amused by the inexplicable pursuits of people from the towns. As well as hearing a few interesting stories we listened to many tedious ones, so the job taught us patience if little else. In those days one could still find a few old people whose lives hovered on the edge of want and who, because they had never mixed with the outside world, kept the old ideas inherited down the ages.

I remember a delightful old woman whose cottage was the end one of a row of five, a mere afterthought of a dwelling consisting of a kitchen-living room and scullery and two small bedrooms reached by a staircase that was little more than a rickety ladder. The whole row was, in fact, a good example of the early type of cottage made with a few baulks of timber and a load of stones and slates from a local quarry, and as picturesque as the famous Arlington Row at Bibury. It had started originally as a four-roomed cottage and then been enlarged as the family grew by adding to it on each side. Later it had been turned into five small dwellings each with its own front door.

Inside and out there was not a straight line in the whole row. The walls had a slight forward tilt, setting the tiny dormer windows askew. The steep-pitched roof suggested that the roof timbers had curved like the ribs of a boat with the weight of its mossy stone slates. The thick walls of makeshift masonry seemed to be held together by the roughly dressed large blocks of stone used as quoins and window framing and it looked as if it had

grown out of the ground rather than been raised above it by
human hands. In the June sunlight, the front gardens bright with
sweet-williams and tall lilies bordering rows of vegetables, with
a climbing rose spraying its creamy-pink flowers over the end
porch it was as pretty a row of cottages one could hope to see
anywhere. The rose was the old woman's most treasured posses-
sion. As she herself said it was a perfect "bower".

Invited into the cottage, we were given a glass of her elderberry
wine. Whatever it did to our heads, for its sticky sweetness con-
cealed an alarming potency, it certainly lit a small fire in our heels
for when we set out for home we found ourselves walking the
eight miles in record fashion.

It was some years before we visited the village again. Remembering our promise to call when we were in the neighbourhood
we went to find the old woman. To our dismay the old cottage
which had looked so gay and bright with its pot plants and clean
lace curtains had degenerated into a hovel taken over by the family
in the adjoining cottage, and now housed wood and broken
furniture, strings of onions, garden tools, old baskets and sacks and
all those other oddments necessary to a countryman's existence.
But the rose still flourished around the battered door, a foam of
delicate creamy-pink with vagrant streamers spreading bronze-
green leaves over the small dirty windows.

A young woman answered me when I knocked at the cottage
next door. "Poor old soul! How she managed all those years I
don't know! To be honest, it was a mercy when she went.
Always going on about the good old days. But what did they do
for her? Living in a place not fit for animals. . . . We're moving
into a council house as soon as it's ready. They're going to pull
the Row down. Good riddance, I say!"

"It's a pity about the rose," I said.

She nodded. "You'd be surprised the folks who stop to admire
it. It's too old to transplant but I'm taking a cutting. It's the one
thing about the cottage I shall miss."

The Row was not pulled down after all. Like many another it
became the country home of townsfolk. A retired business man
from Birmingham bought it. Retaining only the outside shell he
completely modernized the interior, putting in central heating
to defeat the damp and new fireplaces of modern antique design

which never smoked when the wind was in the east as the old ones used to do. The garden patch in front where vegetables and flowers grew side by side is now a neat lawn bordered by white painted posts and chains. The pink climbing rose by the door with its main stem as thick as a man's wrist still flowers gracefully but not with the abandon it did when the old woman emptied her slop pail over its roots each morning.

I made the acquaintance of the new owner who was proud to show me how he had transformed the old cottages into a pictures-que residence. He confessed he was disappointed about the rose.

"I was careful it wasn't disturbed when we put in pipes and the new door. But it doesn't flower like it did when I first saw the cottages and wanted them. In fact it was the rose which made me decide to buy. It was magnificent then. Those old cottage gar-deners knew some tricks about rose growing that never get into the gardening books," he said rather sadly.

I had a sudden vision of a hard-headed business man who had fallen in love with a rose. The slight irritation I had felt at seeing the door tricked out with a ship's lantern and a brass Georgian door knocker faded away. Nor could I tell him why I thought the rose had lost its exuberance. How could I mention slop-pails when I had just been shown the magnificent new plumbing he had installed!

"I could have built a new house with the money I've spent on this one," he remarked. "I did think of pulling it down and using the land. I even went as far as getting a good architect to draw up plans."

"Why did you change your mind? Was it because of spoiling the look of the village with a modern house?"

"No. It was a small thing really." He gave me a shrewd look as if weighing up my possible reaction. "I had faith in the archi-tect. He followed all the latest developments in his profession. He had a Continental reputation and I respected his business sense. When he took me to see a new kind of partition walling he'd installed in his own house I expected to see a modern place, like you see in the magazines; you know the kind of thing, winged roofs and walls of glass, but it was an old mill he'd done up, picturesque as they make them. I decided that if an old house was good enough for him with his profession and good business sense an old house was good enough for me. I asked him, of course, if he would have preferred a house he'd built himself."

"And what did he say to that?" I asked.

"Only that old houses had something . . . like antique furniture . . . . that pleased him . . . and if kept in good order did not lose their value."

There was little new building on the Cotswolds during the last half of the nineteenth and the beginning of the twentieth century. If anything the villages declined, owing to the slump in farming and the new "poverty" of the land-owning classes. This was the period when loads of the old stone slates were removed from barns and farm buildings to be replaced by sheets of corrugated iron, because the slates could be sold for a good price, when wood panelling was taken from the interiors of old houses and went to America along with many a piece of old furniture from farm-house kitchen and parlour. In a few cases whole cottages were carefully taken down, the stones numbered, and then re-erected on the other side of the Atlantic to please American millionaires in love with the quaintness of the Cotswold countryside.

It was the time, too, when mansions too large and expensive for one family to keep up were sold to become schools or the homes of wealthy financiers, people who in many cases disregarded or did not understand the responsibilities which had always gone with the house and land and who had no roots in the countryside. Those mansions which could not find a buyer were left derelict for years, mouldering away in parkland given over to cattle farming.

Many of the old cottages fell into decay. Owing to the slump in farming as well as the use of labour-saving machinery fewer men were employed on the land and families migrated to the towns. As Bernard Shaw once said, the nineteenth century was such a disaster for the common man that anything would be preferable to another century like it, and this applied far more to the country than to the towns where if a man had no work there were more opportunities of finding new jobs.

Because of the lack of employment the rash of small houses and bungalows built by speculative builders which invaded other parts of the country between the wars barely touched the Cots-wolds. It is only in the last two decades that most of the new build-ings have appeared. The bungalows vary from the flimsy commonplace to solid structures of stone or artificial stone which look as if they will stand Cotswold weather for many years. Having been built singly on any site available their situation in relation to the rest of the village is not always happy, but their gardens are bright with flowers from spring to autumn.

The council houses are usually grouped on a hillside or hill-top and, with the later ones at least, a serious attempt has been made to fit them into the landscape. They are usually built of artificial stone, and this product, a mixture of crushed limestone and cement, is moulded into blocks a little larger than a brick, their pale grey colour lacking the warm tones of the natural stone. We have yet to see how they will weather. These stone bricks are cheaper and quicker to handle than quarried stone and can be laid by semi-skilled men, whereas the true stone needs experienced masons trained in handling it. It is this new building material which has been the reason for the opening up of many Cotswold quarries, so that once again one can hear the chink of metal on stone within their precincts.

I did find one cottage in one of the Ampney villages being made of natural stone and I asked the mason, a handsome contented-looking young man, where it had been quarried. He shook his head. "This is old stone from a pulled-down cottage. We clean it and use it again. Hard as a rock," he said, tapping a piece with his trowel so I could hear it ring. He pointed out a pile of stone his mate was preparing, chipping away the grey weathered surface to expose the fresh yellow core within.

"Better than the new stone bricks. It's pricey, of course. This kind of job always is. It's the time it takes."

"You enjoy working with stone?" I asked, remembering the many builders, estate agents, and the quarry owners who sold stone for crushing that I had worried with my questions about new stone buildings on the Cotswolds, and how they had all said emphatically that stone from the quarry was uneconomic, inefficient for the job, and disliked by the masons or stone-brick layers.

"My dad and granddad and his before them were all stone masons. My great grandfather had his own quarry. Now we buy up ruined cottages. They say there's no place for the small family business nowadays and we haven't had any take-over bids for ours, but we get by," he assured me with a twinkle.

II

SOME ANCIENT COTSWOLD ROADS

THE ancient roads of Cotswold can be roughly divided into three types: prehistoric ridgeways, the Roman roads, and the lesser roads and lanes, many of them of Saxon origin, branching off the main highways to the villages and hamlets situated in the valleys and in the folds of the hillsides near the springs, brooks and rivers. All these roads intermingle and overlap in places, for the Romans took into their system of military highways any lengths of the old trackways useful to them, while the Saxons when they penetrated into the Cotswolds naturally used any available road: in later battles for supremacy amongst themselves the trackways and the Roman roads were the only possible routes along which they could move their fighting men.

The ridgeways keep to the top, or just below the skyline, with prehistoric earthworks and burial mounds signposting their upland journeyings all the way. They were evolved out of the coming and going of men and beasts seeking the driest, safest and most open way across the country when most of the lowlands were treacherous marsh or primeval forest. On the whole they were amazingly direct and where they go off course it will be found, if one explores them in the field, that the deviations make for easier travel, either by avoiding a steep ravine, a boggy spring-head or some other obstacle not obvious on the map. Long after the days when the men and beasts who had trodden out these green ribbons across the upland turf had been forgotten, when the surfaces of the Roman roads had fallen into ruin and Saxon and Norman invaders had conquered and settled, these roads were still the driest and most direct routes across the hills.

Monastics riding from manor to manor to collect their dues, wool merchants and clothiers going about their important business between London and the market towns, packhorse trains carrying fleeces and salt and woven cloth, pilgrims and pedlars

and minstrels all used them when the valley roads were deep in
mire or dust. Later, when the turnpike roads came into being, the
toll system helped to keep them alive; by using the old green
tracks Welsh drovers and shepherds could avoid payment of tolls
as well as find a quiet passage and a soft going underfoot for their
beasts. Flocks of sheep in their thousands must have passed along
them in slow nibbling fashion on their way to and from the great
sheep fairs at Stow and Cirencester. Many of the old tracks came
into general use again in the coaching era when lowland roads
were impassable in bad weather.

Nature seldom destroys a green road as long as it is in use. The
hoofs of the sheep help to preserve it, treading the turf into a close
springy mat. When the surface is cut up by the hooves of cattle
the next frosts will crumble the ridges and so fill in the cavities.
Before the Enclosures there were no banks or hedges to define the
width. Travellers naturally went round a miry patch and nature
soon covered the mud with a new surface of tough herbage ready
to be used again.

Modern roads and transport have put the old trackways out of
use as vital lifelines, though parts of them have been incorporated
into modern highways. The unmetalled lengths which remain
today, no longer important in the economy of the country, have
become places where the walker and naturalist can enjoy the
changeless serenity of the hills and the ever-changing beauty of
Cotswold skies. Some of the more remote reaches still serve the
gypsies and diddicoys, the last of the ancient travellers, as camping
places and hideouts from a world which is always moving them
on.

The greatest of these trackways, known as the Cotswold
Ridgeway, is accepted today as being the main artery of communi-
cation across the wolds in prehistoric times, and part of its route
across England from the Bristol Avon to the Humber. Much of it
is still in use, and with interruptions can be followed all the way
in a car, in many cases as a modern road. This makes a fascinating
holiday tour for anyone interested in antiquities, for along its
course are barrows, hill forts and other prehistoric monuments as
well as some of the loveliest hill country in England and some of
the widest prospects of hills and valleys. From Bath it follows for
a mile or two the watershed between the Severn and the Bristol

Avon, and then continues along the watershed between the Severn and the Upper Thames basin. Until it enters Worcestershire at Broadway only three miles is not represented by roads and tracks today.

The Great Cotswold Ridgeway starts off by going roughly north across Lansdown Hill and Tog Hill to just west of Tormarton, the first part of this reach being mentioned in a charter as the Salt Carriers Way. Then on along the ridge above Old Sodbury and Little Sodbury to Hawkesbury, where it has to swing away east to get round a cluster of deeply-cut coombes which lie south of Wotton under Edge. At Starveall it returns to a north-westerly course which it holds to a point about half a mile beyond Calcot Farm before turning east to Chavanage Green. So far much of it coincides with today's main road from Bath to Stroud. The Romans, according to the O.S. map, cut off the corner from Goss Covert to Chavanage Green.

The road winds on above Avening to run between Sapperton village and Sapperton Park. In the spring the new green of beech woods makes this a particularly beautiful part of the route, and in autumn it is lit by the deep red-gold of their dying leaves. It continues north along the ridge between the Duntisbourne valley on the east and the uppermost part of the Golden Valley on the west, and comes to the Roman Ermin Street near Birdlip. Here Ermin Street descends to the Vale of Gloucester, but the ridgeway follows the top of the escarpment, first south of Cheltenham, then east of it to reach Cleeve Common. This, and Middle Hill above Broadway, are its highest points.

From Cleeve Common it winds east, past Belas Knap, the famous long barrow above Winchcombe, to Roel Gate—a junction of several ancient ridgeways—where the view opens out north-westward with the round bulk of Bredon Hill among lesser hills rising from the Vale of Evesham and with the blue Malverns beyond. Leaving Roel Gate it goes north to Sudeley Hill, then north-west to Stumps Cross. It passes south of Snowshill, that remote village of high Cotswold, then over Middle Hill and past the tower on Broadway Hill to the main road from Stow on the Wold to Broadway. And here it leaves the Cotswolds. But it goes on with the hills, and throughout its length it is linked with many another ridgeway and green track.

An offshoot starts from Sapperton, leading up the valley of the Frome to pass Edgeworth, Miserden and Cranham and then descends the scarp at Prinknash. It crosses the swampy ground of the vale by a low ridge, now known as the Portway, to a point where the Severn could be crossed.

The importance of salt in the diet of the Middle Ages when it was used to cure the fish eaten in Lent and the meat for the greater part of the year, the necessity of transporting it from Droitwich, gave the name Saltway to many stretches of ancient roads throughout the country and on the Cotswolds several trackways still bear this name.

One of the longest and most complete crosses the wolds roughly from north to south, leaving Worcestershire for Gloucestershire at Saltway Barn at Hinton in the Green and passing through Toddington and its apple orchards to the foot of the escarpment at Hailes. From Hailes, near the tiny church once a Chapel of Ease for visitors to the Cistercian Abbey of Hailes, it ascends steeply to Salter's Hill, a height of some 800 feet, and from there it keeps to the hill-tops until it falls to the Thames valley near Lechlade.

It continues a little west of Sudeley Castle park walls to Hawling, a remote village consisting of a church, a manor house and a scattering of cottages, and then on to Salperton, another small upland village with a big house. As a footpath the Saltway here loses itself in the Park. From Salperton it runs east of Hazelton, crossing the old coach road not far from Puesdown and then it must have followed the line of the Northleach to Cheltenham highway, branching off at Hangman's Stone as a by-road lined on one side by a grove of beeches until it comes to the Foss a mile south of Northleach. This is high, undulating country, once open sheepwalks in the days of the Northleach wool-men but now under the plough. Camps and barrows are on every side of it, Roel Camp, Penhill Camp and a tumulus east of Salperton, another by Hazelton Grove.

One finds the name again at Saltway Farm below Crickley Barrow, and with the Coln valley below on its right it becomes a minor road, stone-walled and grass-margined. Above Lamborough Banks Barrow the road forks, the metalled by-way going south to Ablington, while the track of the Saltway goes on in a south-easterly direction to Bibury Farm. Only when it has crossed the main road from Aldsworth to Cirencester does it begin to descend gently to Coln St. Aldwyn, and here the hills are left behind as it enters the Thames valley at Lechlade. A deviation must have gone very near to Chedworth, for Domesday Book records that "a portion of the profits of the manor of Chedworth were derived from the toll of salt which came from the hall".

Other Saltways not so easy to trace today except in short lengths came from Droitwich through Pershore and Toddington to Winchcombe and then climbed to the hill-tops, while at Salperton another branch went south-west to Cirencester. Just north of Toddington another descended the hills past Stanway to the Guitings and on to Lechlade via Bourton on the Water.

West of the region the most important one entered the Cotswolds near Chipping Campden, went on to Stow on the Wold by the top road to Sezincote, and from Stow followed the upland road to Church Icomb, Idbury and Widford to Bampton. Eastward it came into the hills to follow the escarpments from Birdlip to Stroud, Wotton under Edge and Old Sodbury.

For the greater part of their routes the Saltways followed earlier trackways and ridgeways as well as Roman roads, treading out a net-work of loop-lines and branches to villages and manors as the need arose, as all old roads must.

One of the famous named roads known to us is Buckle Street. It comes to the north Cotswolds along the Bidford, Honeybourne and Weston Subedge road, climbing out of the Vale of Evesham up the steep side of Saintbury Coppice and forming the east boundary of Saintbury parish. Here it is a rough track known locally as Buckle Street Lane. It begins its upland journey south by Broadway Hill and never touches village or hamlet until it comes to Bourton on the Water. It seems natural to suppose that it once continued to Northleach and Cirencester, but beyond Bourton the site is impossible to trace in the rushy water meadows of the Windrush and Dikkler. It must have served Salmonsbury Camp above Bourton. A barrow just off the by-road to Northleach parallel to the Foss and Norbury Camp west of Farmington may point its direction, especially as this by-road goes on south of Northleach to an ancient meeting place of tracks at Crickley

Barrow. O. G. S. Crawford believed Buckle Street ended at Bourton. To quote from his *Long Barrows of the Cotswolds*, "a prehistoric date can hardly be denied to such tracks as Buckle Street, which is accompanied by barrows from Willersey Hill to its termination at Bourton on the Water". He gives a list of barrows on the way, two on Willersey Hill, one long and one round, and five round barrows including one called Salter's Pool Barrow.

The first mention of Buckle Street is in a charter of 789 when it is called Buggildstret. Another name is Buggildway, and it has been suggested that the name was derived from Burgild, daughter of Cenwulf, King of Mercia from 789 to 819. It would be pleasant to think that Burgild, like the Welsh Helen of the Mabinogion, bride of the Emperor Maxen, inspired the making of roads but there is no evidence beyond the name to prove that this was her road. In a charter of 967 it had become Bucgan Street, and from this the name evolved down the centuries into the Buckle Street of today.

Buckle Street passes through some of the highest reaches of north Cotswold. Near Broadway Tower it is more than a thousand feet and continues at this height until it comes to Cutsdean Hill. For the six or seven miles between Broadway Hill to where it crosses the Stow-Tewkesbury road a mile west of Ford it is in the very heart of Cotswold. Passing Snowshill and Seven Wells it goes on past the old quarries where stone for roofing tiles used to be dug. Below the Stow road the Windrush villages are a mile or so to the west; eastward the lonely hill village of Condicote is more than three miles away. It comes within half a mile of Upper Slaughter by the Wagborough Bush tumulus. Imperceptibly it has fallen from the 1,113 feet of Cutsdean Hill to 700 feet at Wagborough Bush, and it continues to descend until it meets the Foss, the Windrush and the railway at the entrance to the waterside road leading to Bourton on the Water.

The Welsh Way can be linked together by lengths shown on the one-inch O.S. map from Fairford to a few miles north-east of Cirencester. Welsh Way is only another name for a British trackway, "Welsh" being the name given to the Britons by the Saxons. In that sense any of the ancient trackways might be called "Welsh Ways" and many fragments of old tracks known today can be linked to Wales only by the most devious routes. Two other tracks of that name outside Cotswold come to mind; a drove on the Wiltshire downs under Walker's Hill in the vale of Pewsey and a road near Northampton leading to Banbury, which is a continuation of the Great Cotswold ridgeway on its route to the Humber.

The name, however, did come to apply to the Welsh drovers of a later date, for they helped to keep the tracks in use when they brought their cattle along them to the London markets. Welsh cattle drovers are still remembered on the Cotswolds. Near Snowshill, where an old track crosses Campden Lane, there is a spot still called Welshman's Corner by local people, and in the south Cotswolds there is a Calfway Lane—a drove road for many years which gave its name to the village of Chalford where it crosses the Frome. And these are only two of the reminders to be found of the traffic in beasts from Wales to Southampton and London.

The Cotswold Welsh Way leaves Fairford at the river end of the town and for nearly all of its eight or nine miles to Perrot's Brook it is a broad, spacious road. In places it is forty feet wide from hedge to hedge or wall to wall, and it has a tarred surface all the way, except for a mile and a half west of Barnsley. The grass verges on both sides often exceed the width of the surfaced strip.

For the first two miles the trees in the hedges and on the skylines are the heavy-topped elms of Thames valley country, but the road is slowly rising all the time and when it comes to the cross-roads at Sunhill it has climbed some 360 feet. It is a quiet road, direct but not dead straight, undulating gently from one shallow shelf to another. After Sunhill one knows the valley clay has been left behind by the plants of the waysides, veils of traveller's joy misting the thorn thickets that hide the crumbling stone walls.

Still mounting the road runs straight for over a mile to Ready Token, that place of cross-roads with groups of old chestnut and beech trees in the triangles formed by the road junctions. Here there is a large dignified Cotswold house and a cottage or two serving it, as well as a jungle of legends about highwaymen and strange burials in a nearby wood which I have never been able to disentangle. It looks the kind of place around which strange tales gather. The Welsh Way crosses the line of Akeman Street, where

a roadman once told me it was impossible to dig without finding
Roman coins and shards of Roman pottery, and then falls between banks of woodland, rising and dipping until it drops to
Barnsley where it is deeply sunken between high banks topped
with ash trees.

At Barnsley it must now be followed outside the park walls
and along the wide village street; the original course was deflected
when the park of Barnsley was made. Just beyond the inn a steep
tree-shadowed lane climbs to the ridge and now the Welsh Way
becomes a secret, hidden lane, narrowing as it falls to a damp,
coppiced bottom and then climbing once more between sloping
flanks to the uplands. This is the loneliest and most open part of
the Way until Smith's Covert cuts off the views from the north.
Ruts and hollows worn down by centuries of wear and weather
show where the northern fringe of the road was taken in when the
Covert was planted.

Beyond the wood at the top of the ridge wide grass margins,
flowering in summer with native lime-loving plants and edged
with thickets of thorn, hazel and wayfaring trees, give the road
its full width again, but it soon becomes a tarred road once more
with wide views over low stone walls. It makes a characteristic
swoop between trees to Perrot's Brook and the Churn valley. At
Perrot's Brook an old bridge, with low flat-topped parapets, its
grey stones patterned with moss and lichens, is just the place for
contemplative idling, for here the river is wide and shallow, with
crowfoot spreading dark feathering leaves beneath the water and
islands of white cup-shaped flowers opening to the sun. The width
and shallowness of the water here suggests this was once a fording
place for travellers before the bridge was built.

Across the bridge the road now winds upward to cross the main
Cheltenham-Cirencester road at the Bear Inn, and still climbing
gently attains its greatest height, becoming a true upland road,
sometimes bordered with windbreaks of ragged woodland or
opening out to the view. The complexity of ridges converging
and diverging, the narrow valleys and hidden folds it must pass
to reach Gloucester and the Severn make it difficult to follow
today, but after the high country above the Duntisbournes it can
only be deduced by a chain of footpaths, lanes and tracks corres-
ponding in places to parish boundaries and signposted by tumuli

and earthworks. Many reaches have been lost and some are debatable, but it seems reasonable to suppose it continued to a crossing of the Severn and into Wales.

The White Way can still be followed as a minor road from Cirencester to Winchcombe, with a good surface except for a mile or so between Chedworth and Withington woods. The only village it passes through is Compton Abdale and it is a ridge road all the way apart from the steep slopes in the deeply-cut area of Chedworth and Withington, and it passes through some of the highest unspoilt country, particularly near the northern scarp.

Some authorities would claim the White Way as a Roman road, and it must have served the Romano-Britons as a route between Corinium, the Roman villa at Chedworth and the cluster of villas above Winchcombe. Its unswerving line for the first six miles out of Cirencester supports the claim, and it is likely that during the Roman occupation it was straightened and made more direct, but its position on the ridge and the tumuli it passes also point to its being in existence before the Roman legions came to Britain.

It runs north to south and in medieval times was one of the Droitwich saltways. Many of the Gloucestershire manors are recorded in Domesday Book as owning salt pits and springs in "Wiche", identified as Droitwich. It mounts out of Cirencester with the same northward thrust as the Foss on its right and the main Cirencester-Cheltenham road on its left, keeping to the ridge above the valley of the upper Churn. For the first quarter of a mile out of Cirencester there is a striking contrast of Cotswold stone to be seen, for it passes some new houses of cream-coloured stone on one side while the old grey lichen-encrusted park walls on the other give a splendid illustration of how the stone weathers. When the parkland has given way to hillside fields and a skyline fringed with dark woods there is a sudden view of the grey roofs and walls of Baunton in a fold on the left, one of those Cotswold glimpses which show how beautifully the villages fit into the hills. Baunton's little church is dedicated to St. Christopher, the patron saint of travellers, and many a weary traveller on the White Way must have welcomed a sight of the village telling them they were getting near to Cirencester and the hospitality of its inns.

Bagendon church

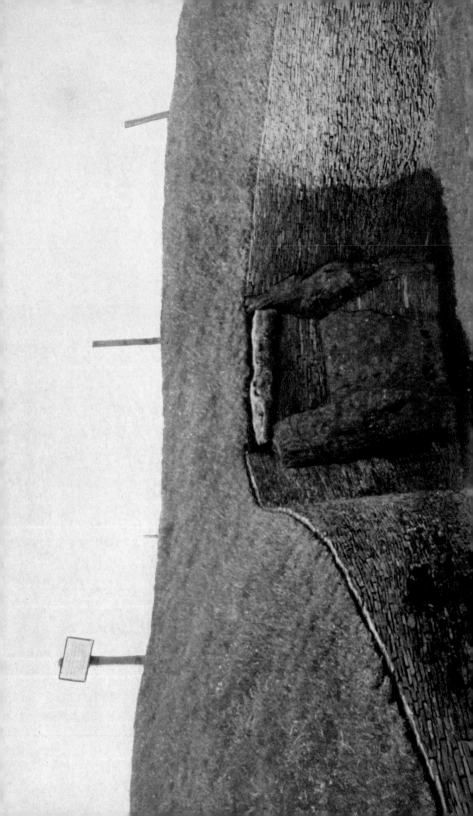

In its second mile the road crosses the Welsh Way and then comes into another long open stretch with a line of tall pine trees making a dramatic windswept picture on the bare ridge. As it comes to Nordown there is a magnificent stone barn with two cart porches high enough for a loaded wagon to pass through, a barn that tells of the bounty of the surrounding fields as clearly as the litter of a discarded airfield farther along the road tells of the famine of war. Old maps show that long before the airfield was built there was an isolated six-went way on the hill-top, a meeting place of tracks in early days.

The track falls abruptly as it enters the dark centre of the Withington and Chedworth woods and then in switchback fashion first up and then down it arrives at Compton Abdale at the bottom of the hill at the wide cross-roads of the village. It passes a spring of tremendous force and volume gushing out through the open mouth of a stone crocodile into a large stone trough covered with moss which also gives the crocodile a strange green beard. The crocodile is one of the many instances on the Cotswolds where a piece of carved stone adds a delightful touch to a delightful village. At this spring travellers on the White Way long before there was a village must have stopped to drink.

The road snakes upward, past the Oxlease quarries and White-hill Farm, and whether the farm was named after the White Way, the salt carried on it in medieval days, or the colour of the road when it was a dusty white track I have never discovered. Still climbing it comes to Roel Gate cross-roads and the highest part of its journey. To the left can be seen the dark plateau of Cleeve Cloud, West Woods in the hollow under it, Humblebee Wood below Belas Knap coming down the skyline in a sharp fall.

As one goes on under the outer walls of Sudeley Park, the Malverns and the rounded bulk of Bredon can be picked out between the nearer hillsides. Between the great beeches of Sudeley Hill the White Way leaves the hills for the "fat" valley, as the Romans called the Winchcombe region some fifteen hundred years ago when they took tribute of corn and wool from its fields and sheepwalks. Its Cotswold journey is ended. As a saltway it would continue to Toddington, Pershore and Droitwich; as a trackway link up with the great ridgeway going towards Broadway and beyond.

3

Belas Knap long barrow

No portrait of the Cotswolds would be complete without some mention of its Roman roads, for unlike the trackways which scored deeply into the hills they were raised above ground. Excepting London, Cirencester showed the most important network of radial roads in Britain. Sometime between A.D. 54 and 68 it was created as a tribal centre for the Dobuni, the southern entrance situated on Ermin Street and a northern gate at the junction of Ermin Street and the White Way. Akeman Street, coming up from Bath, or as some experts believe from Exeter, crossed the town from west to east, while the Foss Way met Akeman Street a mile north-east of the city.

Ermin Street, coming north-west from Silchester, crossed the Kennet, the Thames and then the Churn at Cirencester. Its sixteen miles from Cirencester to Gloucester is a splendid example of a Roman road still in use with a very pronounced agger or embankment in places as high as five feet. It has all the directness one expects from a Roman road, except for a light turn at Daglingworth and another in a northerly direction to keep to the high ground and so avoid the deep valleys running to the west by Syde and Brimpsfield. A short alignment soon brings it into its true course again before it comes to the Edge at Birdlip.

To ease the steepness of Birdlip Hill it comes down the main escarpment as a zig-zag. At the foot of the hill, from Great Witcombe to Gloucester, it is still followed today by the A417 road from Hucclecote to Wotton Pitch. The main road's westward turn from here shows how the Roman road had been originally directed to Kingsholm, north of the city, where Ostorius Scapula made a base for the Second Legion and where a new crossing of the Severn half a mile to the south-west superseded the one at Arlingham which had served travellers on the Cotswold ridgeway in prehistoric times.

The Foss is one of the more puzzling of the Roman roads. Collingwood suggested that it might have been formed along the line of an early occupation boundary soon after the Claudian invasion, it being the custom for the frontier to be accompanied by a road for use in troubled times. The other main Roman thoroughfares in Britain followed natural routes, routes that today are still largely followed by our own main roads, but the line of the Foss is straight and unnatural, much of it being used for minor roads or lanes, and it has no essential place in today's road system.

The Foss leaves Bath by the north gate and coming to Batheaston climbs steeply to Banner Down. From Banner Down to Huntershaw the road is raised some five feet or more, and most of the way to Nettleton across high country the agger is conspicuous. After passing the R.A.F. station at Colerne it winds to cross the deeply-cut wooded valley of the Duncombe Brook, and then goes on to Upper Wraxall. After a slight turn on the high ground near Mountain Barrow it keeps a direct course until it comes to Nettleton Scrub, where extensive evidence of Roman settlement, including a temple, has been found.

Crossing another deeply-scored valley near Nettleton Scrub the agger is no longer visible and the line is a damp green lane. It crosses another steep valley at Gatcombe before coming to Grittleton where for a mile it becomes a wet green lane again. Near the end of this lane where it crosses a small brook the metalling can still be seen and a large flat stone some four feet square is probably the cover of a culvert. After this for a mile or so the Foss is derelict. About a mile south of Easton Grey a by-road branched from it north-westward passing close to Easton Grey House.

For over seven miles now the Foss becomes a green way, with remains of metalling visible here and there, but with no agger, suggesting a different kind of road construction. It passes Long Newnton, near Tetbury, where a foot-high agger is once more to be seen. At Foss Gate, after a short piece of overgrown lane, a very large agger, some thirty-three feet wide and nearly four feet high appears, and this continues until it is lost in another R.A.F. station on the high ground near Jackaments Bottom. A section excavated at Culkerton Wood near this point showed it to have been made of alternate layers of limestone slabs and sandy gravel.

The exact course is now in doubt but it can be picked up again east of the green lane running under Tetbury branch line railway bridge to continue to Cirencester with a fine agger over six feet in some places and a deep hollow along its south side, the remains of a scoop-ditch from which the material was taken to build up the road.

The Foss leaves Cirencester by Querns Lane and Lewis Lane and runs north-east to Hare Bushes Lodge where it meets Akeman Street. Akeman Street branches east at this point, but the Foss goes

due north upon an agger of six feet or so in places and with no
hesitation as to its course. Near Ragged-hedge Covert on Baunton
Downs an alignment sighted north-east to Stow is interrupted to
avoid coombes running to the south. Not far from Calmsden a
zig-zag was made to ease the crossing, and the old embankment
can be seen beside the present road as it rises to the hill-top. The
road coincides with parish boundaries continuously until it reaches
Bourton on the Water.

Just beyond Northleach the road now bends, but the agger is
visible in a field with a stone wall along it. To facilitate the crossing of Broadwater Bottom about two miles from Northleach
another slight deviation from the straight occurs. Farther on, as
the road descends beyond Stow, near the village of Broadwell,
a portion of the old foundation behind a railing at the roadside
used to be exposed to view but this seems to have disappeared.
When Donnington is left behind the agger can be seen once more
as the road goes on to Moreton in Marsh where it becomes the
wide main street of the little town. From Moreton it goes out of
Cotswold country to Leicester and Newark to come to an end at
Lincoln.

Akeman Street leaves Hare Bushes Lodge on the outskirts of
Cirencester and goes direct to the meeting place of roads at Ready
Token as a metalled road. Leaving Ready Token it comes in about
a mile to Coneygar Farm and here the agger can be seen in the fields
as a wide stony bank. It passes Coln St. Aldwyn and enters Wil-
liamstrip Park with the agger still visible, leaving the park at the
east lodge. For a quarter of a mile it runs on a narrow terrace in the
valley of the Leach and then crosses into Oxfordshire. For two
miles or so Broadwell Grove takes up the line. Beyond the Grove
it is not so easy to follow, but a length of cart track and a line
across stony fields takes it on until it becomes recognizable again
near Asthall. It has now left the Cotswolds if not the oolite
country to go north of Oxford and join Watling Street near St.
Albans.

When the Romans left Britain and the roads were no longer
kept in repair the vulnerable places such as culverts and bridges
soon began to decay. Even if the native Britons knew how to
repair them they did not trouble once their masters had departed.
Except for lengths which happened to serve a settlement the roads

were abandoned. Four hundred years is no time at all in the life of a green road, but a neglected made road can be ruined in a few years.

Though part of a general plan, first of conquest and then of settlement, one thing to be remembered is that the roads were not all constructed at the same time, a fact which helps to explain their peculiar lay-out at Cirencester. Though we invariably think of them going rigidly straight what we really mean is that they consisted of short alignments varying in length according to the kind of terrain they passed over. On a flat plateau, for example, the straight lengths were longer, being more easily sighted; broken country or an indented escarpment needed shorter alignments.

In the early years of the Saxon settlements each family was an independent economic unit with little need to travel about the country. They were not interested in the Roman roads. But they did find them useful in some places as boundary banks, and as time went on, and the Saxon homesteads developed into well-defined areas eventually to become in many instances the parishes we know today, these old boundaries, mentioned in Anglo-Saxon charters, remained as useful sources of information about lost reaches of the old roads.

III

BAGENDON

BAGENDON is a tiny village enfolded in the Churn valley some three miles north-west of Cirencester, and the way to it is not on any important through route. It has a few pleasant houses and cottages sheltered by trees and woodland, but most visitors who turn off the A345 into the minor road to the village come to look at the little church.

This has its own charm and mixture of styles. The main fabric is now mostly Perpendicular but the Norman arcade and font point to its origin. The base of the tower is also Norman, the saddleback roof a later addition. The way the building fits snugly into the hillside against a backcloth of trees and a dormer window inserted in the roof of the nave give it a look of domestic rather than ecclesiastical comfort.

A few visitors also come to look at a series of broken earthworks, a puzzle to antiquarians and archaeologists for many years. It did not occur to anyone until 1935 that they might be all that remained of the tribal centre of the Dobunni, and then it was only an archaeological hunch which remained unproved until 1956.

County historians and local antiquaries from 1712, when Sir Robert Atkyns published his *History of Gloucestershire*, to the beginning of the twentieth century continued to believe the tradition that Roman Cirencester had been built on the site of the headquarters of the native Dobunni. The tradition persisted until 1956 when Mrs. Elsie Clifford proved it wrong by finding the old site at Bagendon, one of those instances where tradition has been found unreliable unless one remembers that a few miles or a few centuries do not apply in that real but shifting world.

One reason why the earthworks at Bagendon were never considered seriously was the fact that as long as anyone remembered they had been subject to inundation, and it seemed improbable that a native town of any importance would be found in a place liable to be flooded after periods of heavy rain. The geological formation of the area with fuller's earth between a capping of Great Oolite and a lower strata of Inferior Oolite encourages over-flow springs, and at Bagendon floods were evidently a visitation expected by the inhabitants in bad weather. In the church the unusual height of the six steps above the nave leading to the altar was planned deliberately to keep the altar above water when the nave was flooded. As much as two feet of water has been known to cover the nave for many days together.

Today water still fills the ditches of the encampment after heavy storms. This, however, is due to the road just below the site across the valley acting as a dam and having no opening large enough to carry away the volume of water coming down the valley in flood time. Anyone having had experience of the sudden heavy rain storms of the Cotswolds will appreciate this fact. In pre-Roman days when the Bagendon earthworks were made this road did not exist. Through the centuries the heavy silting of the ditches due to the fuller's earth spreading out with the water-flow disguised the depths of the ditches, but before the road was made the silting would not have been a serious problem to the Dobunni inhabitants.

The position of most of the pre-Roman sites of tribal centres in Briton were known, but even the memory of the site replaced by Cirencester when the Romans moved the Dobunni to a new town was entirely obliterated. By the time the village of Bagendon had grown up about the little Norman church scrub and woodland had covered one side of the ancient defences and parts of others had been broken by gravel diggings. The silting up of the ditches also helped to remove all semblance of an important fortified settlement.

Rudder, in 1778, wondered if the earthworks might have been the scene of a battle between the West Saxons and the Britons, and this suggestion was later published as a fact in the Rev. G. E. Rees's *History of Bagendon*.

After Rudder had seen the earthworks he reported: " . . . south-eastwards of the church in the fields are two considerable entrench-ments fronting each other, one of which extends for above a quarter of a mile down to a place called Barrow's Bridge in this place . . ." He went on to record two or three barrows nearby in which had been found spearheads and other warlike weapons.

Barrow's Bridge is the old name for Perrott's Brook. Part of the course of this brook forms the parish boundary of Bagendon. Apart from such speculations by Gloucestershire historians, each attempting to fit the earthworks into his own pet theory, little was known about the Bagendon site.

When, however, in 1951, it was decisively proved by cutting a section through one of the last remaining portions of the earthern ramparts at Watermoor in Cirencester that the defence banks once surrounding the city were no earlier than A.D. 175–200 discussion about the pre-Roman headquarters of the Dobunni again became archaeological news. It was then that Mrs. Elsie Clifford, the Gloucestershire archaeologist, who knows her county and its history intimately, remembered how some twenty-five years before she had found a piece of Romanized pottery in a gravel pit at Bagendon on the top of a stone construction or platform she had taken to be the metalling of a Roman road. As the existence of a Roman road on this spot was unlikely the inconsistency roused her creative curiosity, a faculty possessed by all good archaeologists, leading her to clear the debris of many years from the now disused gravel pit. In this process sherds of Belgic pottery were found for the first time.

In 1953 Mrs. Clifford decided to excavate at Bagendon, and from 1954 to 1956 worked on the site. It was not long before she knew she had discovered the lost town of the Dobunni, the town the old antiquarians had called Caer-Cori which ceased to be occupied when the new Roman Cirencester became Corinium Dobunnorum. Not that one must think of Bagendon, or any other tribal oppidum, as a town with an urban ground plan. Caesar's description of a British town was of an area of rough country fortified by earthen ramparts, the enclosures containing a considerable population of people and animals who spilled over the ramparts except in times of danger. It is significant that Bagendon was well served by two ancient trackways, being near the junction of the White Way and the Welsh Way, both of which led to other ridgeways crossing the Cotswolds in all directions, with the ancient ford at Perrott's Brook for the river crossing.

Mrs. Clifford had seen the stone construction in the gravel pit some twenty-five years before the excavations at Watermoor proved that the Cirencester rampart was Roman. In 1932 this gravel pit was still being worked, and about this time the Rev. G. E. Rees wrote in his history of the village that an oblong stone-pitched platform once nearly 1,000 square yards "had two cavities on opposite sides from which had been recovered animal bones, sherds of coarse pottery and fragments of burnt wood". What happened to these things is not known. He also tells how part of the bank was destroyed when the garages and stables of Withy Close were built, and during the course of the building two skeletons were found with an earthenware pot on the inner slope of the bank. The dating of this pot was said by the British Museum to be of the first or second century when it was sent to them for confirmation by Mr. A. D. Passmore, the Wiltshire archaeologist, who had acquired it for his extensive collection. This is believed to be the Belgi pot marked "Bagendon" which was amongst his gifts to the Ashmolean Museum some years later. The Ashmolean Museum in its turn presented it to Cheltenham College Museum as being of local interest and during the storing of the museum's contents in the last war it disappeared.

The gravel pit area with its peculiar stone platform was the obvious point at which to begin the new excavations.

The site covers altogether some 200 acres, and is in the neighbourhood of Bagendon village and the adjoining hamlets of Perrott's Brook and Woodmancote. On the east it is bounded by Cutham Lane leading to Woodmancote, on the west by the valley escarpment, on the north by North Cerney and on the south by the Welsh Way. It lies on a south-facing slope protected from northerly weather by rising ground, with a subsoil of gravel. There is plenty of easily-worked limestone available for building. On the northern side a strong spring rises, and sherds of Early Iron Age pottery found near its mouth show it may have been used by the people who lived on the site. There was open land just beyond the ramparts for pasturing their animals, and bones of roebuck found in the digging suggest there was hunting available. In fact it had everything a settlement could desire.

With the aid of air photographs and a close survey of the area the many pieces of ditches and banks so bewildering to the casual eye soon took shape. This winning back from centuries of obscurity a lost and forgotten settlement must have been a rewarding experience as each earthwork was plotted, the line of the lost portions established, and it became apparent once more as a unified system of entrenchments comparable in size and importance with any other known tribal centre or oppidum in the country.

As the work proceeded it became plain that the people of Bagendon lived in half-timbered huts, probably roofed with thatch of reeds or straw, with foundations and floors of large, close-fitting stones. The presence of daub with wattle impressions suggests that the interiors were as comfortable as the homes of the rural workers of much later centuries, as anyone who has studied the housing conditions of farm workers and cottagers in the nineteenth and early twentieth centuries would agree.

Rotary querns bear witness that corn was grown and a great number of large earthenware storage jars were found. Ox-goads suggest ploughing by oxen. The Belgic Dobunni also kept flocks of sheep, and pottery spindle whorls and triangular loom weights show that wool from the sheep was spun and woven into cloth. The impression of sandal nails on the floors implies they wore sandals, probably made of hide from home-killed pigs and cattle. The vast quantity of animal bones found shows that farming must have been on a large scale, and as many of the bones are of mature animals some kind of winter feeding must have been available. Pottery for home use was made near the site.

The diet of the inhabitants consisted not only of home produced products such as grain and meat but of mussels and oysters brought from the coast. Their wine came in amphorae, while butt beakers, some of Continental origin or from southern England, suggest that beer, also, was one of their drinks.

Bronze and iron brooches and pins to fasten clothing, rings, bracelets and beads for personal adornment, and bronze mirrors were found, and these articles appear to have been made on the site and show the metal-workers to have had a high degree of skill and knowledge of their craft. They made many types of brooches, including one of delicate and intricate workmanship now to be called the Bagendon brooch, as the design appears to have originated at Bagendon.

The minting of coins was one of their major industries, and the smiths used a touchstone to assay metals. The one found at Bagendon is only the second to be recognized in this country. They also understood a highly technical process of refining whereby silver is abstracted from lead, the lead, of course, coming from the Mendips and probably brought along the great Cotswold ridgeway leading to the Mendip Hills. The smiths at Bagendon also worked in copper and produced amongst other things an early form of Sheffield Plate.

Pottery from Italy, red-glazed ware from southern Gaul, fine glass from Egypt or Syria were imported. These luxuries and the distribution of coins minted at Bagendon point to considerable trade between the Cotswolds, the south of England and the Continent. All the evidence shows that the Belgic Dobunni were a powerful and wealthy tribe, with many of the refinements thought to belong to a later age. Mrs. Clifford writes in her account of the excavations that they were governed by kings "who number no less than seven".

When between A.D. 50 and 60 the people of Bagendon left their valley-side home to live in Cirencester and the kings, in their own right, were no more, they took with them cultures and skills equal in quality to the Romanization imposed on them. Many of the Roman luxuries they knew already, the wine and oysters, for instance, and evidence that the smiths continued to ply their crafts can be seen in the Corinium Museum today in the iron work and the many small bronze objects whose charm and freshness still delight us.

The archaeological evidence found by Mrs. Clifford brought to light a tremendous amount of new material for future study and comparison, as well as releasing expanding circles of new ideas. This is no place to go into their significance to the professional archaeologists, who have now proven facts instead of probabilities to use in their endeavour to bridge the gap between the two worlds of history and protohistory. Writing of Mrs. Clifford's work in his introduction to her book, *Bagendon: A Belgic Oppidum*, Sir Mortimer Wheeler ends with the words: "We are her debtors". Might I be allowed to say respectfully, on behalf of those of us who are not archaeologists but who love the Cotswolds and its story, that we also are her debtors for opening up this fascinating new chapter in its history, and bringing to life those shadowy Dobunni who have haunted its hills for so many centuries.

IV

THE ROMAN VILLAS

APART from their roads the Romans did not alter the face of the Cotswolds permanently. The valley-ward drift, the greatest change Britain had undergone since it was first inhabited, as Collingwood points out, came later with the Saxon settlers who preferred the river valleys and the heavier soils of the lowlands. During the Roman Occupation it was still the lighter soils of the hills and hill slopes which were cultivated, with two systems of settlement existing side by side, the villages on the hills and larger isolated homesteads of the wealthy Romano-British land-owners.

It was these independent land-owners who acquired the Roman way of life, their homes being rebuilt as the Roman villas whose remains can still be seen, with drainage, under-floor and wall heating, tessellated pavements and painted, plastered walls. Rome expected the owners of these establishments to become urbanized, with duties and interests and often a domicile in the new tribal centres, or towns, knowing that having adopted a new way of life and found it to their liking the native leaders could then be depended upon to be loyal to Rome.

This is not to say the villa system is a Roman concept. Caesar found the Belgae living in isolated farms, and archaeological evidence shows that this kind of establishment existed as far back as the Bronze Age, the villa being only a Romanized adaptation of land tenure in being long before the Romans came.

The Cotswolds must have been a paradise for the villa-owners. Over fifty sites are known though the majority are not visible today. "Beyond doubt," wrote Haverfield, "rich men must have been common as weeds round Cirencester during the Roman Age." Excavations have shown us and are still showing us a good deal about their architecture and furnishings. Coins found show that most of them were at the height of their prosperity in the fourth century, and a few new villas were built about this time. These, it would appear, were never finished or at least not furnished with the elaborate mosaic floors and plasterwork, while pottery and household goods are fewer and of a poorer quality, suggesting that the rot had already set in. The late villas, also, are not in such good positions. The earlier ones are always found on sheltered and well-drained hill-sides with a good water-supply available. The sites were chosen with care, where the soil was fertile and with plenty of timber at hand.

The most splendid villa on the Cotswolds must have been the one at Woodchester near Stroud, famous for the beauty and size of its pavement. Nothing is to be seen above ground now but at intervals the great pavement is exposed for a few weeks and then carefully covered again, first with fine sand and then with earth. Lack of money to build a protective roof and pay a custodian means it must lie hidden most of the time.

The villa is believed to have been destroyed towards the end of the fourth century and signs that fire caused its final extinction have been found. From that time the remains became slowly submerged, though some of the stone served as a local quarry. It is supposed that a Norman church built near the site of the main hall was largely constructed from material taken from the ruined villa. An archway of this church still survives, with typical Norman carving on its jambs and lintel. This is more delicately patterned than most Norman doorways in the Cotswold churches.

As the centuries passed all knowledge that a mansion had ever stood on the spot was forgotten and a churchyard was made over part of the site. When vaults and graves were being dug the diggers found their work obstructed by the exceeding hardness and toughness of the cement foundations of the pavement and so the villa was discovered. Two of the earliest records of it come from the *"Additions"* to Camden's *Brittania* by Bishop Gibson in 1695, and from the notes of Dr. Richard Parsons, county antiquary and historian and Chancellor of the Diocese of Gloucester. He wrote " . . . not far from Minchinhampton at Woodchester, famous for its tessariak work of painted beasts and flowers, which appears in the churchyard, two or three feet deep. in making the graves". The fact that he describes the pavement as "painted" suggests that he had not looked very closely at the mosaic, for their soft colourings come from natural colours of the stone and brick used in composing it.

Both the two eighteenth-century county historians, Sir Robert Atkyns in 1708, and Samuel Rudder in 1779, mention the pavement. To quote Rudder: "Many coffins were placed upon it but it has been frequently broken through at the request of some families who desired to have their friends interred at a greater depth". Some of the eighteenth-century tombs to be seen in the churchyard have acquired an antiquarian charm of their own today, including a group of the famous Paul family, originally clothiers of Woodchester, which are to be seen on the extreme edge of the pavement surrounded by iron railings.

The exact date of the building of the villa is not certain and from the extent of the foundations it has been argued that it was either the country house of a Romanized Briton of great wealth and importance or the official residence of the Roman Governor of the Province. There is no definite evidence to support or disprove either of these theories, unless the fact that one of the beasts represented in the pavement, a stag, looks like a later more clumsy insertion into the circle of jungle animals. It is hard to believe the stag was part of the original design because it breaks into a meticulously executed border. It is the only animal native to Britain represented, the others being circus animals better known to the Romans than to the British. It is an intriguing theory that a stag would be more acceptable to a Romano-Briton than a Roman Governor. It might even have been his crest. Alternatively it could be argued that a Roman Governor learned to hunt the stag in Briton and acquired a passion for the chase. It is one of those small mysteries which add a touch of piquancy to the whole problem.

The site was excavated by Samuel Lysons in 1793, soon after a portion of the pavement had been exposed by the digging of a vault for a certain John Wade of Pudhill. It aroused Lyson's antiquarian fervour and probably his indignation and he continued his uncovering and assessing at intervals for the next three years. In 1797 he published his *Account of the Roman Antiquities Discovered at Woodchester in the County of Gloucestershire*, and this account is the chief source of information about the villa.

Lysons seemed to think that Woodchester was associated with Ostorius Scapula or Vespasian, both of whom were great builders in the west between A.D. 47 and 54. Troubles with the

Silures across the Severn were long and protracted, and from the escarpment near Woodchester the Severn and the ways leading from it to the Cotswolds can be overlooked. He pointed out the tactical value of its position as a station defending the Severn crossings, a theory which favours the building of the villa early in the Occupation.

No evidence that it was a military station has been found, and this theory does not fit in with the well-known fact that villas were not built until the second phase of Romanization, that is after new towns or tribal centres had been made and the tribes brought down from their hill-top forts to live in them. On the other hand recent evidence at Fishbourne in the east of the county has shown that beneath a Roman villa of the usual type wooden buildings once existed of an earlier date, and as Woodchester has never been the subject of an extensive excavation more evidence to date it may one day come to light. It seems more likely, however, that the date of its building was around A.D. 117–138, the designs and patterning of the mosaics being those generally prevailing about the time of Hadrian, who was known to have built in the west during his stay in Britain.

The villa was of the true courtyard type and shows a great degree of Roman influence in its design. It possessed two large courts surrounded by buildings covering 500 by 300 feet. The main residential part surrounded the inner court with colonnades on three or four sides. The foundations of at least sixty-five rooms were revealed. As well as the usual features and amenities it contained a large hall floored by the great pavement, and from the hall passages covered with mosaics led to rooms on either side. At the height of its prosperity it must have been a magnificent mansion, and though the manner of its building belonged to Rome the stone of its foundations, walls and roofs came from quarries in the neighbourhood.

The great tessellated pavement covered a square of forty-eight feet ten inches, surrounded by a strip of red brick tesserae. Its subject is the Orpheus legend, though there is little left of the figure of Orpheus. The story was a favourite one with the designers of mosaics for it makes the introduction of almost every living thing possible. There is another example in the Corinium Museum at Cirencester which came from Barton Farm near by.

The craftsmen worked with some kind of trade pattern book but varied the arrangement of conventional border designs as well as the centres according to size and individual taste. The smaller the cubes of brick and stone the more fluid and intricate the design, and the great pavement at Woodchester is made of half-inch cubes and originally contained about a million and a half of them. The preparation of the foundation was thorough; without human interference it could have lasted another two thousand years.

First a three feet bed of gravel resting on a foot of coarse rubble was laid down, and over this a bed of coarse cement eight inches thick. Finally the tesserae were embedded in a cement of a finer quality. Under the pavement was a heating arrangement of flues crossing at right angles joining box flues placed in the walls. One wishes they had been less conscientious when grave-digging so that more of the pavement could have been left to us.

All the materials came from the surrounding countryside, the blue lias from the valley of Gloucester, the white oolite from the Cotswolds, the dark brown stone from near Bristol, the light brown from Lypiatt. The red cubes are of fine brick. All were highly polished, probably with a piece of fine tile, to give a smooth shining surface and bring out the natural colours of the stones. These are part of its charm and give brightness without being garish. Moreover they have kept their colour through the centuries. The fact they have been covered for so long may have helped them to retain their freshness.

Within the outside strip of red brick is a wide ornamental border of labyrinth frets and interlacing and twisting braids, and the making of the borders alone must have been a highly skilled job for they contain every variation of fret and braid possible. Inside the border are twenty-four compartments arranged about a central square and ornamented with more geometrical figures. Intricate as these patterns are, they are but the framework of the main design contained in a series of concentric circles. The outer circle, twenty-five feet in diameter, is formed by a Vitruvian Scroll with pointed foliage, a rolling pattern emphasizing the circle it borders. It is completed by a mask of Pan with a beard of leaves.

Inside the broad band are various beasts on a white ground, free and lively in conception, including a bear, a leopard, a stag, a tigress and a lioness. A boar, an elephant and a dog are now des-

Sudeley Castle

troyed. I regret the loss of the elephant particularly, for all the animals, except the stag, give the impression that Orpheus has roused them into the particular grace and movement of their kind, and an elephant under the influence of his potent music must have been a splendid sight. The animals are about four feet long and separated from each other by trees and flowers.

Another circle bordered by a band of acorns divides the animals from the birds. A peacock, a dove, a hen, and a cock pheasant can be identified, the pheasant scratching its head with its foot. A fox has intruded into this circle of birds, an amusing touch making the designer of the creatures seem less remote to us. According to Lysons' drawing there was also a circle of fish and sea-creatures surrounding a star-like figure at the very centre of the pavement. The four figures outside the circles showed female figures, nymphs or Naiads, but most of these are missing. It is the mixture of geometrical patterns, mythological figures and the natural objects which gives the whole conception its fluid and lively grace; the rigidity of the frets accentuating the flow of leaf and animal forms pacing the outer circle.

The mosaics found in the other rooms of the villa are smaller, consisting mostly of frets, mats and stripes. The most interesting small pavement was one showing Bacchanalian figures as well as two boys holding an offering of fruit with the inscription *Bonum Eventum* underneath. Bonus Eventus was a rural god of husbandry who came to preside over the eighth day of the Roman week, and was, perhaps, one more favoured by the Britons when they were obliged to take over the Roman gods.

Pieces of coloured marble from the Continent, broken Doric columns, fragments of decorated Samian ware, blue and green glass, iron knives and daggers as well as a large number of coins of the "lower" empire were found during the excavation. A more recent find was a later coin of Theodosus I (A.D. 378–395). Two pieces of statuary, one part of a group of Cupid and Pysche in white marble, the other a draped statue of the Goddess of the Moon with a bull at her feet, are now in the British Museum.

Chedworth Villa, in the valley of the Coln, now belongs to the National Trust. Because of the pleasant way the site is preserved it has little of the melancholy and desolation of a ruin and has become an open-air museum, an excellent example showing how

4

Tessellated pavement, Chedworth Roman Villa

the buildings fitted snugly into the sides of a coombe. It is almost entirely surrounded by woodland and is so secluded that it would be possible to pass within a few yards or so of the entrance without being aware of it. It is served by two Roman roads, the Foss some four miles to the east, and the White Way, an ancient track taken into the Roman road system, coming across the uplands from Cirencester; the ways to it from these two main thoroughfares are through narrow winding lanes bordered by rich parkland.

The site faces east, but the bite of the east wind is tempered by woods and undulating slopes so that it gets the full power of the morning sun without the usual rigours of an east-facing slope. A spring gushing forth from a bed of fuller's earth provided a plentiful pure water supply, and both the fuller's earth and the inexhaustible supply of water were an asset when at a later date fulling became part of the villa's economy. Behind the villa rise steep hills so that the fields must have been in front where lies the narrow valley of the Coln with its flat bottom.

Like Woodchester, Chedworth was of the courtyard type, three sides of the square being surrounded by buildings with the other side left open to the east. The rooms at the west end of the north wing were originally a large set of baths. Another set of baths were built later in the west wing, so that one does get the impression the inhabitants spent a great deal of time washing or bathing. The villa was discovered in 1864, when a gamekeeper digging out a ferret also dug out some tesserae. The remains of the walls have been roofed with stone tiles belonging to the original building found during the excavation, and their dark age-old surfaces lightened with orange and silver lichens add greatly to the harmonious aspect of the whole. The mosaic pavements are protected by unobtrusive shelters.

As at Woodchester local stone was used. One can see the reservoir, the heating system, the workshops and store-rooms of the north wing where two semi-circular buildings are thought to have housed the smithy, and the enormous vats which may have been used for fulling. Not far away overlooking the river there was a temple. Trying to reconstruct the way these people lived some fifteen hundred years ago it would seem they had almost everything required for a healthy and happy life: an idyllic setting, country sports and pleasures, fresh home-grown food, the amenities of urban civilization not only a few miles south at Cirencester but in the villa itself. Life was probably hard enough for the slaves and field workers whose labours made this possible but one hopes that even for them there was some compensation in the beauty and security of their surroundings and the fertility of the fields and animals they tended.

It must have seemed to those villa occupiers who never doubted the might of Rome that it was a way of life that could go on for ever, and they built accordingly. Yet the seeds of decay were there from the beginning, not only because their safety depended upon those to whom they were subordinate but because the produce from the country estates had to feed the towns, the administrators and the craftsmen, in fact an ever-growing non-food producing population growing larger as the towns increased.

There was also a villa at Withington, just north of Chedworth, a village with its own historian, H. P. R. Finberg who, in *Roman and Saxon Withington*, gives not only a scholarly account of its beginnings but puts forward a fascinating theory about the sub-Roman period there. We are apt to take it for granted that the Romano-British settlements were entirely extinguished by Saxon raiders and settlers because of the lack of evidence of Celtic survival. Mr. Finberg suggests that it was unlikely the Saxons could have built up a civilization from scratch which within three hundred years was strong enough to withstand the continuous Viking assaults. To him it seems more likely that when a group of Saxons had defeated a local chief or caught him unprepared they would take over a going concern, sometimes a village in full working order or one from which the inhabitants had fled. Where the villagers remained it would only be a matter of different masters and would their condition be very different from what it had been?

Once the possibility of continuity is admitted it could explain many things, for instance the fact that Withington, to quote Mr. Finberg, "a villa-estate in the fourth century, came through the sub-Roman period with its boundaries intact, to become episcopal property in Ethelred's reign".

Mr. Finberg opens out a new field of investigation and the case he puts for continuity is a strong one. It would help to close the gap in our knowledge of the years between the ending of the villa system and the rise of the Saxon settlements.

V

CIRENCESTER

CIRENCESTER is the capital of the Cotswolds, in feeling, appearance and because of its position at the entrance to the hills. All periods of its growth, from the time it began as Corinium Dobunnorum some fifteen hundred years ago to its status as a modern market town of today can be seen within its boundaries. It is one of those towns where the old gives grace to the new and where building styles of Gothic, Stuart, Georgian and early Victorian exist side by side in harmony and the usual town fringes of indeterminate fashions do not take up too much of the picture.

Cotswold is renowned for the charm of its little towns, some hardly more than villages today. A good deal of this charm comes from their miniature compactness, being small enough for the traditional Cotswold dwellings to have an intimate relationship with each other as well as with the landscape, though this also means they can be more easily destroyed by indifference or vandalism. Cirencester, despite its much wider spread and a population of over 11,000, has been able to keep its coherence, though I wonder how long it can continue to do this under modern conditions.

The Roman Cirencester grew up at the crossing of the Churn, first as a small military station and then as an important meeting place of roads as the Romans advanced westwards. When the Romans had established themselves firmly in Britain it became an urban community, the market centre for the wool, corn and other commodities produced by the many large Romano-British estates in the surrounding countryside. By the end of the second century the earthern rampart enclosing its 240 original acres had been superseded by stronger defences of stone facings. When Diocletian reorganized Britain for imperial administration into four parts it became the capital of the province of Brittania Prima, and one of the most highly Romanized of the twelve tribal capitals.

A visit to the Corinium Museum in Park Street and a little imagination will soon bring to life the Roman Cirencester enclosed within its ramparts and guarded by four main gates, the temples, baths and public buildings whose colonnades were finished with Corinthian capitals, carved cornices and pillar shafts, its handsome houses belonging to the wealthier citizens. As well as the sculptured stones, altars and mosaic pavements, the tiles stamped with the marks of local tileries, the personal articles, such as brooches, glass phials for medicine and cosmetics, tiny bronze birds and animals, iron tools and cooking utensils give more intimate glimpses of its daily life.

Here, also, are the tombstones of two Auxiliary cavalrymen, Genialis of the Thracians and Danicus of Indus' Horse, dating the time when it was a military station. The carving on each tombstone is of a mounted soldier piercing a prostrate foe with his spear, a stock subject for memorials of this period to be found in many museums. Natalis and Biticus, the inscription tells us, put up the stone to Dannicaus according to his will, and being his friends doubtless mourned for him. The tombstones are more than evidence by which archaeologists can date the beginning of the city; they conjure up a picture of two young men travelling into strange lands to die and be buried far from home and represent many a soldier's fate throughout the centuries.

The middle of the sixth century saw the end of Corinium as a peaceful prosperous town. Left without the protection of the Roman legions the inhabitants were once more exposed to encroaching raiders. The Britons rallied under Ambrosius Aurelianus for nearly fifty years, but by this time the Roman administration of the city had come to an end. The town existed uneasily, always under the threat of the Saxon hordes, with the population swollen by refugees from the unprotected villas seeking what they hoped was greater security within its walls.

An entry in the *Anglo-Saxon Chronicle* under the year 577 states: "In this year Cuthine and Ceawlin fought against the Britons and killed three kings, Conmail, Condidan and Farinmail at a place called Dyrham; and they captured three of their cities, Gloucester, Cirencester and Bath". A body of a tall Saxon warrior complete with shield and spear was found buried under the broken tessellated pavement of one of Cirencester's houses, and it tells its own story of the massacre and the desolation which must have followed the sacking of the town. The remnants of the population and those who crept back to its ruins when the Saxons moved on must have led a miserable existence amid the ruins and broken monuments of Roman imperialism. The desolation was made more complete by the flooding of the waters of the Churn at the lower end of the city turning it into a marsh, the "water-moor" now giving its name to a modern street. It is thought this damage was done deliberately by the raiders to destroy the town.

By 628 Corinium had become Saxon Cirencester, as we know from records of a battle there between Cynegils of Wessex and Penda of Mercia when the men of Wessex were defeated. Hereafter the Cotswolds were incorporated into Mercia.

The strategic value of Cirencester's position as a gateway to the hills near an important junction of main roads and trackways kept it from becoming entirely abandoned, and with Bath and Gloucester it revived in some form as an administrative centre, for the Seven Hundred of Cirencester form a distinct unit of the Cotswolds. There is a tradition that a monastic house was founded in Cirencester during the brief reign of Egbert (829–830) but no traces of its buildings remain today. The Danes spent a whole year at Cirencester in 879 at the invitation of King Alfred who, as he was unable to conquer them, preferred to know where they were while he was gathering his forces elsewhere. The *Anglo-Saxon Chronicle* describes a great assembly of magnates there at Easter 1020 under King Canute and it seems to have been used as a place for conferences and assemblies between the king and the important men of his kingdom. Apart from this there is no mention of the town in the history books until after the Norman conquest.

Once the Normans had established themselves the commercial life of the country began to expand. It was natural that Cirencester should gradually resume its urban character. Domesday records a market there, and in the twelfth century the ancient White Way, known as "the way leading from Cirencester to Campden", was once more busy with the transport of wool and corn from the hills and salt from Worcestershire as it had been in Roman times.

One of the best ways to see the town is by a series of leisurely explorations about its streets, and I found that the best time to do this was in the evening when the traffic had died down sufficiently to make it possible to look and linger without being jostled by shoppers and tourists or run down by impatient drivers. The hour or so before dusk in the earlier months of the year before the holiday traffic is at its peak is a good time and also the hour before the town is fully awake in the morning, if one can be sufficiently interested so early in the day. Both have their particular appeal; the evening light can soften as well as reveal the scars and renovations of ancient buildings, while morning freshness has its own illuminating moments. The evening, perhaps, for those who prefer a more romantic setting.

Taking Cirencester's history century by century one can follow it from the twelfth century onward as one wanders about its streets, and with a study of the church fabric and monuments build up a picture not only of the town's history but see how it is woven into the history of England and the part it played in its making. The rectangular street plan of Roman times was obliterated in the dark days after its sacking by the Saxons, and the names of the streets which slowly took shape through the centuries tell their own story, Dyer Street, Castle Street, Abbot Street and Shoe Lane.

There is nothing left of the castle built by William Fitz Osbern and his son Roger where Matilda was known to have stayed and where she received the Bishop of Winchester in the hope he would recognize her claim to the throne. Stephen, after his escape from Bristol where he had been held by Matilda's men, completely destroyed it in 1142, and even its site is disputed. A few years later, however, a great abbey church was consecrated in the presence of Henry II, and though this was pulled down at the Dissolution there is still a relic to be seen in Grove Lane, the delightful gateway known as the Spital Gate at the northern end of what was once the abbey precincts. It gives a medieval touch to the town and makes one regret the loss of the whole range of abbey buildings.

The abbey was a wealthy one and its powerful abbots controlled most of the town's trade, with a right to coin money and to a seat in Parliament. A good deal of the abbey's wealth came from wool, for Cirencester, like Northleach, Campden, Fairford and other Cotswold towns was a centre for the wool trade and the abbey owned the sheepwalks for miles around. During the reign of Edward III it was recorded that the abbot could store 20,000 bales of wool in his sheds, and he had his own merchant's mark used in his capacity as wool merchant. This can still be seen on the parish church.

Cirencester being an important religious centre there was much journeying to and from the town by kings, nobles, ecclesiastics and their retinues. The tower of the church is said to have been built with treasure taken by the townsfolk when the earls of Kent and Salisbury marched from London and came to Cirencester during their move to restore Richard II to the throne after his deposition by Henry Bolingbroke, soon to be Henry IV. The earls were captured by the abbot's men and the townsfolk together, and in this affair, at least, town and abbey were united, though in town matters there was continual friction between them, the abbot insisting upon his rights as lord of the manor and the towns-people anxious to be free of his demands, rules and regulations giving them little say in the town's affairs.

Evidence of the wool and clothing trades can be seen in almost every part of the town. Thomas Street contains the Weavers Hall, founded in the fifteenth century for poor weavers and dedicated to St. Thomas of Canterbury. It is a sombre-faced building whose fabric of layered brick-shaped stones is relieved only by the larger blocks of stone around the narrow splayed windows and the flattened arch above an iron-bound nail-studded door. Its sole ornament is a small carved figure above the door, too worn by time and weather to be identified but probably representing St. Thomas.

Coxwell Street, an unspoilt little thoroughfare between Dollar Street and Thomas Street, still keeps its tall old mansions, for-merly the homes of prosperous wool-staplers, and the smaller gabled houses of their workers. Part of a house at the Thomas Street corner was once a wool warehouse, all of these buildings belonging to the days when owners and workers alike lived in one community near their work.

As one would expect the wool trade, foundation of Ciren-cester's medieval prosperity, has left its records in the parish church. The Trinity Chapel was built partly for the Weavers Company and partly in honour of Richard, Duke of York, by two of his men, Sir Richard Dixton and Sir William Prelatte around 1430, but why the two combined I have never been able to discover. The chapel also contains a brass showing an old man in a gown with a pair of shears above his head and a dog at his feet. The inscription reads:

> In Lent by will a sermon he devised
> And yerely precher with a noble prised
> Seven nobles he did give ye poor for to defend
> And 80L to XVI men did lend
> In Cicester, Burford, Abingdon and Tetburie
> Ever to be to them a stocke yerely
> Philip Marner who died in the year 1587.

Though we do not know the names of the men who were lent the money it is likely, judging from the places where they lived, that they were wool merchants or men engaged in a subsidiary trade who were suffering from the decline of the export of wool to the continent.

This brass has been taken as evidence that "Cissester" and not "Cirencester" is the correct pronunciation of the town's name, once a source of argument amongst Cotsallers. Generally one finds the inhabitants shorten it to "Ciren", a slovenly abbreviation unless one imagines its first letter to be an S.

Other merchant's memorial brasses in the church are to Reginald Spycer and his four wives, and to Thomas Page and his wife. Thomas Page, like Thomas Fortey whose brass is in Northleach church, left money for the mending of roads, a pious and worthy cause in those days. As merchants travelling between the towns of the Staple they must have suffered from the mire, dust and potholes of the unmetalled roads and understood well the need of such charities.

The Fleece Hotel's timbered front, now much restored, stands out amongst the Georgian façades of the buildings surrounding the Market Place as a reminder of the medieval wool trade as well as a reminder of an earlier more picturesque style. Most of the house fronts date from the time when the congested huddle of stalls, shops and narrow alleys which had sprung up between them were at last cleared away, some five hundred years after the towns-people had protested bitterly to the abbot about the nuisance of the encroachment and which, we are told, the abbot encouraged because of the tolls he exacted from the traders. Butter Row, Butcher Row and others whose names tell their own story were entirely demolished and the Market Place began to take shape as the broad handsome thoroughfare we see today.

The town is rich in eighteenth- and early nineteenth-century houses, for this was the period when wool-staplers and clothier employed their wealth to build themselves mansions on earth unlike the earlier wool-men who used their surplus to rebuild churches as a means of ensuring mansions for themselves in heaven when they died.

One of the most handsome is Gloucester House in Dyer Street, and another of equal dignity on the corner of Silver Street is now occupied by Lloyds Bank. Its solidity and restraint has no trace of the empty pomposity often found in Georgian houses erected at the end of the period. Built in 1720 by a wealthy wool-stapler this must have been one of the earliest in the new Classical style to grace Cirencester's streets. Semi-circular recessed arches curve over the pilastered windows, a balustrade between a double string course runs the whole width of the building between the ground floor and the first storey, and the central block of the building juts out a little, accentuating with its pediment the perfect proportions of the horizontal and upright lines.

Doorways and porches of Classical design add a touch of graciousness to many of the streets around the town's centre, such as the doorway in Gloucester Street which has a simple scroll embellishment on jambs and lintel, and over the lintel an oval tablet most delicately carved. Mr. A. F. Kersting's book of photographs of the town shows these details admirably and his book makes a good guide for a first visit.

One of the pleasures of a leisurely stroll round the town is that the buildings of many periods are not set out in distinct localities but stand side by side as they evolved naturally out of the chances and circumstances of the times. Cecily Hill, leading to the gates of Cirencester Park, is a delightful example of a juxtaposition of styles in a single street, and it has the added attraction of being a haven of quietness away from the roar of through traffic. On each side of the broad street are houses of various dates, some with long, narrow front gardens giving it an air of mock eighteenth-century rusticity as of town ladies dressed as milkmaids. One seventeenth-century house has had a "Strawberry Hill Gothic" bow window added to its original front, and beside it stands a large Georgian house with a Doric porch. I cannot make up my mind if the Barracks, looking like a monstrous toy fort or sham castle after the manner of its kind, which stands on the right of the park gates disturbs the placid scene or not. The discovery of new weapons of war of the last fifty years has made its design more than ever a symbol of medieval military power and completely taken away its once menacing aspect. Time now gives it a quaintness, and one can imagine antiquarians will be soon discovering it as a treasure to be preserved along with deserted railway stations and other Victoriana for the benefit of posterity. A television aerial on its roof proves that the inmates are not living in the past.

Cecily Hill was formerly known as Instripp Street, a name which describes its position as a cul-de-sac perfectly but without grace. It was given its present name because a chapel of St. Cecilia formerly stood there, and its new title suited it so admirably the old one was soon forgotten. That it has a pleasing sound I discovered when taking a small boy there who asked me its name as we went to the park. He was one of the children who make up little chants, infant calypsoes as it were, and I was amused to hear him singing softly to himself over and over again:

> Sweet Cecily Hill, sweet Cecily Hill,
> I went with Miss Brill to sweet Cecily Hill.

When I returned him to his aunt at the end of the day she asked him where he had been, for she was a lady much given to asking questions.

"To Sweet Cecily Hill," he replied reluctantly.

"I hope you addressed Miss Hill properly and answered nicely when she spoke to you," she said a little anxiously.

"Oh, she wasn't the kind of lady who asks a lot of questions," replied Richard in the curiously flat tone he used for reproving inquisitive elders.

Cecily Hill comes to an end at the gates of the park, but part of its appeal is the way it appears to continue as the Broad Ride, flanked by wide lawns and magnificent trees and with the dark clustered woods as background and wings. It is a noble park of some 3,000 acres, laid out by the first Earl Bathurst assisted by Alexander Pope and Dean Swift, and encouraged by the wits and literary men, Steele, Gay, Prior and Congreve who came under the earl's patronage. Talk and wine must have flowed merrily in the planning of it.

Pope spent at least ten summers between 1715 and 1725 at Bathurst Park. Where seven rides converge an ornamental summer house is still known as Pope's Seat. But time plays strange tricks with a poet's fame, for when I was there recently a passer-by asked me if I could explain how the Pope came to leave the Vatican and give his name to a summer house in the park. Alexander Pope would have enjoyed writing a couplet or two to provide the answer. It is said that he actually planted many of the trees, but I doubt if he realized the day would come when all the town would be able to wander beneath them. In some of his verses he pokes fun at the tree-planting, but the fact that he could be amusing without his usual bitterness suggests that the rural scene, properly controlled of course by human intelligence, gave him one of the few pleasures of his life.

It was only natural that the activities of Earl Bathurst, one of the first land-owners in the district to try out more advanced methods of farming and to demonstrate the value of the Enclosure Acts to the agricultural world, should be expressed in Pope's verses. In one of his "Moral Essays" published in 1731 he may have been answering indirectly some of the criticism directed against the Enclosures with his descriptions of one

> Whose cheerful tenants bless their yearly toil,
> Yet to their Lord owe more than to the soil.

In another set of verses he plainly refers to the pulling down of part of Sapperton village, some five miles away, in order that more land could be taken into the vast estate.

> Link towns to towns with avenues of oak,
> Enclose whole downs in walls—'tis all a joke!
> Inexorable Death shall level all
> And trees, and stones, and farms, and farmers fall.

It all seems very commonplace to us today, but in Pope's time it must have seemed the most exciting pastime in the world to be a landscape gardener on such a vast scale.

Today as we walk freely along the rides and avenues one can only be grateful that Cirencester Park with its eighteenth-century urbanity and spaciousness is still left to us barely untouched by the commercial speculations of land-grabbing companies who are destructive rather than creative in the manner of the first Earl Bathurst.

Cirencester's wool trade as in the rest of the Cotswolds disappeared in the early nineteenth century, but by this time, being on an important junction of four main highways it had become a coaching station and this helped compensate for the loss. The coming of the railways put an end to this traffic for though two stations were built neither were on main lines.

In 1845 the Royal Agricultural College was opened, a great asset to the town and making it known all over the country as well as abroad. Cirencester then began to develop as a tourist centre and a residential area. The building of a new industrial estate, opened in 1945, and since then the coming of several light industries provides work not only for Cirencester but for men in the surrounding villages, and the airfields in the vicinity have also helped to bring fresh life to the town. Antiquity does not weigh too heavily upon it, nor is it insisted upon so strictly as to quench the necessity of moving with the times and keeping alive and prosperous.

Its finest building, the parish church, dominates the town from many prospects by its splendid Perpendicular tower 134 feet high, and the great porch added at the beginning of the sixteenth century gives the Market Place its most striking adornment. Part of the cost of the porch was paid by the local guilds and at one time it was used as the Town Hall and for other secular purposes. The soft stone used to rebuild its façade in 1836 soon began to need repair, the intricate carving losing its crispness and requiring constant attention. It has since been taken down and put together again, so that it now stands out in lighter tones than the dark grey of the rest of the fabric, showing up the richly fretted carvings of its six oriel windows and niches.

The best time to see it is on a day of brilliant sun and shadow after a storm when the clear rain-washed air makes every detail stand out. There are some who wish to see the church's ancient stones in a setting of green lawns and quiet retirement, but the fact that it is jostled by shops and the busyness of the Market Place does make it part of Cirencester's daily life in presence as well as spirit. One can only blame modern conditions for making it impossible to look closely at it except at night and early morning. The noise and bustle, however, ceases as soon as one enters the dim cool interior, and one is back again in Cirencester's storied past.

VI

DAGLINGWORTH,
THE DUNTISBOURNES AND SAPPERTON

FROM Cirencester Ermin Street rides majestically across the hills to come to Birdlip at the edge of the scarp and then drops down to the vale of Gloucester. Like all main roads out of Cirencester motorists driving along them are urged by the stream of fast traffic to speed on, only to discover they have gone through the Cotswolds and seen very little of them. Several times I have been told by casual acquaintances that there is nothing to the Cotswolds but a few good roads, and that they could not understand what all the fuss was about.

This kind of traveller may catch a glimpse of a church tower or a cluster of grey roofs through a screen of wayside trees but more often sees no sign of human habitation apart from petrol stations, roadside inns or the few hamlets unfortunate enough to be on the line of a main road. To find the villages one must have time to spare and be willing to turn off into the narrow roads branching from the main routes. For those who cannot resist a signpost pointing into some half-hidden way these minor roads can lead to many a charming secluded village and stretch of unspoilt countryside.

Less than forty years ago they were lanes roughly metalled with local stone, white with dust in summer and orange-coloured after rain, the communities they served remote in their hill-folds or narrow river valleys. Even today when town and country are fast becoming one they have not lost their reserve and rural quiet. The less fortunate, that is those reckoned the most picturesque or having some special tourist attraction, though how the selection came about and who made it is difficult to discover, have their privacy invaded by visitors on Cotswold Tours, but as this is a seasonal invasion once the coaches and cars have passed through it is as if they had never been.

These minor roads follow the line of a meandering stream, the contour of a hill-slope or the high park wall enclosing an estate and were not made for swiftness of transport. They evolved out of ancient needs and boundaries as well as being adapted to modern ones as the years went by, and it would be found that there are good reasons for the often erratic nature of their courses if one traced their beginnings and subsequent history in the parish records. This kind of fascinating detective work, however, needs much time and patience.

They are good places for encountering the animal and bird life of a district—a fox or hare crossing the road, an ambling hedgehog, a stoat on the trail going purposefully in and out of the stone walls. One is seldom without yellowhammers or finches to keep one company. They flit along in front dropping a few tinkling notes as they fly, and then lose interest and sit on a bush or wall to preen themselves. A few yards on one encounters another little company and so it continues until the first cottages and farm buildings are reached.

One may be less than a mile as the crow flies from the roaring main road but here is peace and the true Cotswold grouping of farm and farm buildings, church, manor house and cottages. Each grouping has its individual character and has arranged itself harmoniously into the landscape. The newer council houses on higher ground, though often built of reconstituted stone bricks and dark roof tiles to keep them in tone with the older parts of the village, never seem so happily sited. One wonders again and again how the masons who built the old cottages managed to find just the right positions in which to place them. The answer is, of course, that they did not choose them with any conscious planning in mind, but that the quality of the stone and the wide curves of the landscape makes an old Cotswold building, be it the smallest cottage or large house, seem in the right place whatever its situation.

To reach Daglingworth and the Duntisbournes one turns off Ermin Street at Stratton, a mile or so out of Cirencester, a place, as its name implies, of Roman origin, but now a tiny hamlet with a much restored Norman church. The road follows the Duntisbourne stream to its head at Duntisbourne Abbots. This stream, a tributary of the Churn, flows through an open hollow of water meadows and flanking woods with Daglingworth as the first vil-

Cirencester: medieval church;
modern police station

lage after leaving Stratton. There is only room for the stream and narrow meadows on the floor of the valley and the stone cottages and houses are placed on the slope just above. Protected by the hills and in good river valley soil the sloping gardens flourish making wonderful banks of colour in their season against the green meadows and darker woodland.

In the grounds of a gabled farmhouse there is a circular pigeon house of old grey stone deeply stained with the patina of centuries. It has 550 nest-holes and provided fresh meat in winter for the inmates of a nunnery, a cell of Godstow Nunnery in Oxfordshire, which once stood here. It also held an advowson and a small pension out of the rectory of Daglingworth in the twelfth century. The pigeon house makes a charming introduction to this secluded little valley, and I expect the gardeners and farmers of the neighbourhood are glad that it has outlived its original purpose.

The church is perched above the village. Looking back from the top of the little rise leading to it there is a lovely grouping of part of the village in a fold of the valley showing the long lines of dark roofs to perfection. About and behind the church tall trees make a rich backcloth beautiful in all seasons. There are traces of Saxon work in the angles of the east end of the chancel, and some Saxon carvings on the walls, placed there when the chancel arch was taken down many years ago and it was found that the jamb stones were sculptured, and had been reversed in an earlier restoration. One, representing the Crucifixion, shows Christ in a kilted loin cloth in the centre with a smaller figure on either side, one with a spear, the other holding the sponge and jar. It is a primitive, literal rendering of the old story, crude but touching in its simplicity.

By the side of the church is a large, square, plain-fronted house having a row of horseshoes along the base of its front walls, a decoration pleasing to any traveller with an eye for the smaller eccentricities of country life and who likes to invent characters and stories to fit them.

About a mile upstream is Duntisbourne Rous, a tiny village of a few farm cottages in a deep hollow near the ford. In one of the farm buildings is a small two-light lancet window looking as if it came from a lost ecclesiastical building. The church is well above the flood line on a small rise overlooking the stream. Outside it

5

William Grevel's House, Chipping Campden
Cutsdean

appears as a plain structure of unassuming homeliness, its rough hoary walls with traces of Saxon work in its fabric and a low saddleback tower to distinguish it as a church. Within it wears its years and office with grace and dignity. The high narrow nave is enhanced by beautiful roof timbers; a panelled wainscot, the Jacobean pulpit and misericord stalls add a warmth and richness of carved mellow wood. Taking advantage of the slope a small crypt, which once served as a chapel, has been made under the chancel. It is a church with a cherished look.

A tall-shafted cross with the mutilated time-worn remains of the original head is in the grassy churchyard and the eighteenth-century box tombs have the beautifully engraved bronze name plates typical of the district. It is one of those village churches not only placed in a perfect situation but which has an endearing perfection in its miniature simplicity. No wealthy wool-man or titled clothier found it necessary for the good of his soul to add a Perpendicular tower or imposing aisles, no nineteenth-century restorer came to mar its ancient peace. The Norman Rous, or Redhead of the village name, has left no sign of his domination. Its once isolated position and the unimportance of the village has served it well.

Duntisbourne Leer, the next village along the stream, has its waters lapping the doorsteps of some of the cottages, and half a mile on, at Duntisbourne Abbots, one is never far from the sound of running water. Coming to it from the low road by the water-meadows the village can be seen dotted around a bank making an up-slanting village green. At the foot of this green bank the water gushes into a large semi-circular stone trough edged with mimulus and other water-loving plants, and though this is no longer in general use as the village water supply I hope the trough and its water will remain. It is a delightful piece of simple masonry and makes a focal point for the village. From the trough the water falls abruptly to stream level, so that the lower cottages are always within the sound of falling water, and the rest of the village as well, I expect, when the quietness of nightfall intensifies every sound. This lower level of the village is deep in lush greenery and is beloved of blackbirds and thrushes.

The church, high above the water-level, has a saddle-backed tower. One might be inclined to overlook it at first, but a closer inspection reveals belfry lights of latticed stone, and on the church door a lock and key and closing ring made by a seventeenth-century craftsman who wrought his difficult material to show how delicately it could be worked into an intricate pattern. The font with its formalized decoration of leaf and stem is a good example of the transition from the deep-cut abstract Norman design into the more natural forms of the Early English tradition.

When I visited the village in May 1963 several of the old houses and cottages were empty, with lilac flowering above rampant rose-briars and the gardens a wilderness after being left untended for a season or so. A dry-stone wall knocked down to make a garage entrance, a clutter of builders' materials outside, showed they were about to be modernized into rural retreats for retired people and others seeking the peace of the countryside, or for commuters from Cheltenham or Gloucester not many miles away.

A different comeliness is about to descend on the village as it has done upon so many others in the Cotswolds, and with two big towns only a short distance away there are the pleasures of the town to be enjoyed as well as those of the countryside. The change is a paradox of modern life, and as far as it means preserving the old with the aid of the new it is all to the good. If the new villagers sometimes go a little too far in their attempts to reproduce a picturesque old England that never was at least the squalor and un-wholesomeness of many a quaint cottage has been eliminated. If it adds a new kind of suburbia to village life it also brings people genuinely anxious to preserve and not destroy, and people with time to devote to village affairs and interested in old ways and by-gones the average countryman is usually pleased to do away with.

There is, of course, the occasional die-hard ancient holding on to the past like a dog with a very old bone which has long lost its meat. My sympathy is with the ancient whose roots go deep and to whom the present is but a passing show. One of the diffi-culties newcomers to village life discover is the putting down of roots. It is hard to reach any depth if one has not been brought up and suffered in and with a place.

A road from Duntisbourne Abbots goes south-west across high country and in about a mile comes to the Jack Barrow cross-roads where it meets a road going south to Sapperton. This road is on the site of an old trackway which continues as a metalled road to Lowsmoor Farm. The metalled road goes westward but the old trackway kept due south and its traces are lost in the fields. This is some of the loneliest country of high Cotswolds well over 600 feet all the way, dotted with long barrows and earthworks and for the last two and a half miles to Sapperton bordered on the right by the walls, woods and plantations of Cirencester Park.

Sapperton at the east end of the Golden Valley has escaped the industrialization which follows the Frome and the disused canal from Chalford to Stroud in its narrow bottom. The canal was conceived by Lord Bathurst with the aid of Alexander Pope to link up the Severn with the Thames near Lechlade by a waterway thirty miles long, and here goes through the limestone ridge by a tunnel of two-and-a-quarter miles cut into hard rock. The entrance, being in the environs of Cirencester Park, has been ornamented with columns and niches in the Classical style, but is now the haunt of birds and not boats.

Sapperton with its grey stone cottages and church stands on a shelf above a deep gorge with woods and parkland coming almost to its gates. The broad churchyard walk is lined with yews of great age and an ancient cross with a slender headless shaft and steps hollowed by many feet stands by the path. The Church was practically rebuilt in the days of Queen Anne and the interior lighted with large windows of clear green glass and furnished with much well-polished and well-preserved woodwork. It holds the white marble tomb of Sir Robert Atkyns with his effigy holding a book representing his famous history in his hand, the fascinating alabaster tomb of Sir Henry Poole who died in 1616 and is here seen with his wife and family dressed in the elaborate fashions of the day, and a more austere grey stone effigy of an Elizabethan Poole, once lord of the manor. In the churchyard Ernest Gimson lies buried.

To those concerned with English art and craftsmanship Sapperton with neighbouring Pinbury and Daneway should be a place of pilgrimage, for it is here that Gimson had his workshops and lived and worked for the last twenty-five years of his life. These were his happiest and most productive years. By then he had decided the kind of life he wanted to live, the kind of work he wanted to do and where he wanted to do it, and his genius came to full flower in the peace and harmony of a countryside whose aspect contented his spirit as well as his eye.

In his day Sapperton, though only eight or nine miles from Cirencester, was a remote place, the woods of Cirencester Park practically cutting it off from the town on two sides, while on the west and south-west lay the involved hilly district leading to the escarpment overlooking the Severn and the Vale of Berkeley, a district of deeply-cut and heavily-timbered valleys and hill slopes served by steep, narrow, winding lanes surfaced with local stone and difficult to negotiate in bad weather.

The Cotswold building style of steeply-gabled stone-roofed and stone-walled farms and cottages was a source of inspiration to him, not only because of the way they grew out of and were perfectly adapted to the local climate and nature of the countryside but because the pattern of their building had survived from the Middle Ages, satisfying his desire for continuity in the English tradition.

Gimson saw no distinction between the arts and the crafts; he wanted art interwoven with life, to reveal something of the lives of those who created it, and believed that a natural living art could only come about by keeping alive old traditions and developing them, a very different view from those fashionable today. For him rural and domestic uses must be as much linked with the craft as the craftsman himself.

It was natural, therefore, that his interest and understanding was with those older men who had been trained in the skills of their forefathers, who had their roots in regional life and a pride in their daily work. He fervently believed that work must be not only a means of earning a living but should bring happiness and content to the worker, a theory outmoded today when educationalists are concerned in teaching how the increased leisure hours should be spent to offset the monotony of daily work. From the time he came to London in 1886 after an early training in a Leicester art school and architect's office he had been slowly forming this philosophy, to become at last what W. R. Lethaby called "an idealist individualist".

William Morris, Ruskin and Herbert Spencer were the prophets he revered. In London the Barnsley brothers and other members of the Art-Workers Guild became his friends and he soon joined the Society for the Protection of Ancient Buildings founded by William Morris and Philip Webb. Morris made a profound impression upon Gimson which lasted all his life, but unlike Morris he did not express his ideas in public. He was an artist, not a crusader, and expressed his ideas and ideals through his life and work. W. R. Lethaby sums it up in a superb memorial volume printed by the Shakespear Head Press. "Work not words, things not designs, life not rewards" were his aims.

The fact that he pursued his aims quietly and uncompromisingly and with small profit, sharing the happiness it brought him only with a few like-minded friends and pupils and never seeking publicity, kept him from being as well-known to the general public as he was to the connoisseurs and informed lovers of the arts and crafts. That he was a happy as well as a dedicated artist can be seen in his work. A preference for natural over abstract forms shows clearly in the examples of his skill in pure applied ornament, which carry him on in direct succession from those medieval English craftsmen he admired so much.

Today he is best known for his furniture. Some of his finest pieces are in museums, but Gimson would have made no distinction in his work. Whether he was designing a house, a cottage, a memorial cross, a hall for a famous school, or smaller articles of ironwork such as latches and strap-hinges, he gave them all the same intense concentration and care. To him the smallest piece of work was as important as the greatest. That outworn definition of a genius as "the infinite capacity for taking pains" might have been made for him.

But he had something else, a purity of vision shining through everything he did. Though he had a diversity of skills and practised architecture, furniture making, metal work and other allied crafts his designs came within the framework of a single purpose, and this single-heartedness was at once his strength and his weakness. He knew it could only be nurtured by turning his back on London and its disturbing influences of foreign ideas, trivialities and commercial attractions. The quality of his work shows that this decision was the right one for him.

He lies in Sapperton churchyard under one of the great yew trees which line the path to the church. His memorial of two flat slabs of stone with "E. W. Gimson, 1919," beautifully engraved on a small square bronze plate is in the style characteristic of the district, as is shown by the stones from the seventeenth-century onward to the Yarnton family in a group nearer the church door. Beside him is an upright stone to Sir Emery Walker, another friend and associate of William Morris. On the opposite side of the path under another great yew are the tombstones of Sidney Howard Barnsley and Arthur Ernest Barnsley, who were also his friends and fellow-craftsmen.

Sapperton has changed little since Gimson lived and worked there, though over the hill the road to Cirencester is made hideous by the noise of planes taking off. The policeman has a new house of Cotswold stone with a grey-tiled roof in which the architect has skilfully contrived to suggest the gable effect so that its lines are in keeping with the rest of the group of cottages where it stands. Unlike the industrial part of the valley nearer Chalford and Stroud the last forty years have used it kindly.

VII

CHIPPING CAMPDEN

CHIPPING CAMPDEN is the most perfect of the small Cotswold wool towns. In the last decade or so the outskirts have suffered by haphazard building but its heart remains unspoilt, and on the whole its concessions to the tourist trade are discreet. When the cars and coaches have departed the long curving High Street can still give one a sense of wonder that such perfection should have survived: underneath the wonder is the fear of what might be lurking round the corner waiting for an opportunity to destroy its ancient harmony.

The town lies in a long wide valley enclosed by hills to the north, south and west, though as soon as they rise to a height overlooking the town on the north the scarp falls steeply to the Vale of Evesham. On the east it is open to the valley of the Stour. Three ways lead into it from the uplands and the town belongs in spirit and character to the hills.

Unlike most places which need the bustle of human activity to give them life Campden is best appreciated when its famous High Street is quiet; only then the past which made it comes into its own. The High Street shows one architectural incident after another within the unity of the Cotswold vernacular, a tradition taking little heed of the innovations in English architecture developing outside the limestone belt. Having found a style of building in the latter half of the fifteenth century best suited to the local stone it kept its variations within that style. There is only a difference in scale between the largest houses and the smallest cottage until the thrust of the eighteenth century and the Classical revival made itself felt throughout the country.

The stone being porous, steep-pitched roofs were the most practical way of using the heavy stone slates if they were to keep out the rain. The mullioned windows with heavy lintels and labels made the perfect finish to freestone walls. Dormers and gables relieved a plain façade and two-chambered gables with a porch between satisfied a sense of proportion and gave dignity and grace to the larger houses as well as providing the two living-rooms which superseded the small parlour and the large hall of medieval days. When the masons felt need of self-expression there was the stone asking to be carved into the embellishments still delighting us today. That the hoary and darker tones of the slates should weather into deeper tones than the walls, accenting the pointed arches of gables and dormers and conveying the impression of a roof covering as a climax to the whole was accidental, but the harmony has its origin in the use of material native to the region and responding to its influences.

The stone used for the building of Campden came from the town quarry near Horseman's Corner above Westington. The old workings are now overgrown by trees and shrubs, a sanctuary for native plants sown by the birds and the wind and a haunt of jays and magpies. At one time it was a favourite camping ground for diddicoys and other travellers on their way to the fruit- and pea-picking in the Vale of Evesham, and it has that dishevelled gypsy aspect beloved of birds and children. It was here I found my first long-tailed tit's nest in a blackthorn thicket, and my first blue feather dropped from the wing of a jay. It was here, also, we used to pick cowslips more lush than those on the hillsides, and sweet white violets under the hedges.

I once had a strange experience in the old quarry. At the time it seemed heavy with a significance I could not resolve, nor have I tried to rationalize it since. Searching for wild flowers I came upon a small clearing within an inner tangle of shrubs, a clearing I had never seen before. A man sat with his back against the bleached trunk of a dead tree with a dog beside him, a lean secretive-looking animal with rough hair of nondescript colour, a body shaped like a greyhound and a long rat-like tail curled about its legs: it was not the kind of dog a child instinctively stoops to fondle.

The man sat motionless as if carved in wood. In many ways he resembled his dog, for his face was thin and brown and his eyes had the same unhuman quality. An old tweed coat of loud pattern which had obviously been made for a bigger man hung about him and he wore a scarf of brightly-coloured rag tied in a knot at his throat. His dark hair was brushed off his forehead and slicked down like a pelt into his neck. There was a tenseness in his attitude, a concentrated brooding which took all the innocence out of the sunny morning.

The dog gave a low growl as I began to push through the bushes and I saw the coarse brown hair rise along its spine. The man made no sign. He sat there immobile, and I stared at him and then, suddenly afraid, turned and ran, tearing my stockings on bramble trails, stumbling over tree-roots and making as much noise as a stampeding elephant. I do not know why the cracking of dead twigs and the pounding thud of my feet should have increased my terror except that they echoed the pounding of my heart, for I was at an age when making a noise could still be pleasurable, but I do remember the blessed quietness when I reached the haven of the road. I was halfway down the hill before I discovered I had dropped my bunch of flowers, but I did not go back for them. It was many years before I went into those thickets again by myself and then I only skirted the edges to watch a new part of the quarry being opened.

Like other quarries on the Cotswolds the Campden quarry has been worked on and off since the Middle Ages and has been opened again in recent times. To a lover of the region the sound of the quarrymen's tools has its own music, and the new stone immaculate in its freshness looks as beautiful as when time has laid its patina of lichen and age over it.

The oldest house in Campden is Grevel's House in the High Street, said to have been built about 1380. It is the most perfect small domestic building of its period on the Cotswolds with its gothic doorway and two-storied panelled oriel, and one of the most photographed houses in the town. When it was built it was in advance of its times for it was probably the first house in Campden to have fireplaces and chimneys to carry away the smoke instead of vents in the roof, and no doubt many people shook their heads sadly over the folly of newfangled ideas being allowed to spoil the look of the town.

William Grevel, who erected it out of the wealth he made as a wool-merchant, might serve as an example of how the wool trade brought prosperity and a rise in social standing to many an industrious yeoman's family. Being an astute man he profited not only by his trade but by lending money to the king and thus gaining influence at Court. In a tax roll of 1380 he is mentioned as being taxed, with his wife and five male servants, and that he and his son John were pardoned "for all unjust and excessive weighings and purchase of wool contrary to the statute".

John, who was his eldest son, became Sheriff of Gloucestershire and the Marches of Wales, and later Sheriff of Warwickshire and Leicestershire. His son Thomas was made knight of the Bath at the coronation of Henry VII and fought at the Battle of Stoke for which he was made Knight Banneret. Once on the way up the Grevels further improved their position by good marriages. The grandson of John Grevel, Sir Fulke Greville I, married Elizabeth Willoughby, the sole heiress of Sir Willoughby de Broke. Elizabeth was descended through her grandmother from the ancient earls of Warwick, and it was her grandson Sir Fulke III, patron of Ben Jonson and Shakespeare, who rebuilt and refurbished Warwick Castle at the cost of £20,000 and became Baron Brooke in 1621. They evidently kept their interest in the wool trade, for Agnes, the sister of Sir Fulke I, married Sir Edmund Tame, son of John Tame, the wealthy wool merchant who became lord of the manor of Fairford and who built Fairford church.

John Tame is remembered today because of the church and the wonderful painted glass of its windows; William Grevel is remembered because of his house and his memorial brass in the parish church describing him as "the flower of wool merchants of all England". He also followed the pious custom and after-life insurance policy of the wealthy wool-men in helping to rebuild Campden's church, though to what extent he contributed is not known. The church must have been dear to him for when he died in 1401 he left 100 marks for the "new work" and asked to be buried there.

It used to be thought that he built the tower because of the similarity in design of the pinnacles about the west door with those etched on his memorial brass, but as the design is common to the period this is not very convincing; there is stronger evidence for believing he built the north aisle because at one time, according to Percy C. Rushen, the historian of Campden, there were "many mullets dispersed over it", and mullets appear in the Grevel coat of arms.

His brass and that of his first wife Marion now rest on a grey marble slab on the chancel floor in front of the communion rails. It was taken from the nave and placed there to preserve it during a restoration. It may have formed part of an altar tomb situated in the north aisle. The effigies are almost lifesize and lie under a double canopy. In each pediment can be seen his merchant mark, a cross standing on a globe with a streamer attached to the shaft. The inscriptions are placed in French fashion, the husband's beginning under his feet, and those of the wife above her head, each distinct from the other. The close decoration, the crocheted and cusped canopy, the foliated capital of the centre pinnacle, the diapered band and the four shields showing his coat of arms make it plain that William Grevel was more than a country wool-merchant concerned only with buying and selling and must have been a man who enjoyed the refined and more decorative aspects of life fashionable in London and on the Continent.

Three other brasses to Campden wool-men are to be seen in the chancel, having been removed from the floor of the nave when the church was restored. They commemorate William Welles and his wife Alice, John Lethinard and his wife Joan, and William Gybbys and his three wives and their thirteen children. There is no memorial to Robert Calf, who is thought to have built the Woolstapler's Hall about the same time as William Grevel built his house.

The Woolstapler's Hall has never captured the imagination in the same way as Grevel's House, perhaps because it is more austere in appearance with little decoration to relieve its solid façade. The evidence that it was built for Robert Calf consists of a rough coat of arms on a fireplace of its upper room discovered by C. R. Ashbee during his work on the building, which had suffered much disfigurement and abuse during the poverty years of the nineteenth century. The name survives in Calf-lane, a narrow way at the back of the building leading from Church Street to the town mill, and to quote Rushen "it is highly probable that the Calf influence must have been very prominent in the vicinity for Calf-lane to be retained to this day, and it is the oldest personal name-place in the parish".

Like the Grevels the name of the Calf family appears in Campden records going back to the middle of the thirteenth century, but no record that the family lived in the town after the fifteenth century has been found. The Woolstapler's Hall has always been known by this name. There is little doubt that it was used as a meeting place or Exchange for the wool-merchants of the town and their agents.

When the wool-trade declined it had various owners and occupiers, including the Hands family, and for a short time it was called after them. We get a glimpse of it in 1672 when £2 12s. a year, a charity of a dozen of bread weekly to "the poor of the town for ever", was given by William Blackley or Blakeley, and was charged to the premises. William Blakeley "one of the burges of this town" also presented the church with its "fourth" bell in the peal of eight, so it suggests that the building was still in use at that time and had not degenerated into the poor condition from which C. R. Ashbee rescued it.

Keeping as far as possible to the original design he sympathetically restored and adapted it for his own use, and today it looks much as it must have done when it was first erected in the fourteenth century.

Campden's prosperity as a wool town had come to an end by the beginning of the seventeenth century. There were few wealthy residents, the church was in need of repair and the town could not afford to repair it, the endowments of the grammar school had been filched by unscrupulous trustees. The day of the wool-men as the most important merchants in the country's economy was over. It was the mercers and clothiers who now took their place.

It was at this time that Sir Baptist Hicks, a rich mercer of Gloucestershire ancestry, bought the manor and gave new life to the decaying town. An interesting record from Rushen's *History of Campden* shows that Sir Baptist Hicks bought Grevel House with other properties in 1617. It had been sold to a certain John Price by Edward Grevel some fifty years previously, and after this sale there is no other mention of the Grevel family in the Campden records. It may seem a little ironic that so little remains of the splendid Italianate mansion Sir Baptist Hicks built by the church while the fourteenth century Grevel House still remains.

We know a great deal more of Sir Baptist Hicks than we know of William Grevel because he belonged to an age when the pedigrees and benefactions of the landed gentry were written up by writers depending on the patronage of wealthy families. To some degree his career and that of his family followed the same pattern of advancement as William Grevel's. As well as his new mansion in Campden Sir Baptist built a great mansion in Kensington and named it Campden House. It is said that his wife Elizabeth preferred London to country life, and because of this and because his business interests were in the City he spent most of his time there. He did not neglect his country estate, however, and in many practical ways helped to restore the town's dignity.

A list of his benefactions can be found in Stow's *Survey of London*, and these include in detail his many gifts to Campden, including the almshouses and their water supply, a new Market House, church restorations and many smaller gifts. He also put the affairs of the grammar school in order, no easy job as the trustees had destroyed most of the original documents to cover their depredations.

He was raised to the peerage as Baron Hicks of Ilmington and Viscount Campden of Campden in 1628, and when he died a year later aged seventy-eight he was buried in Campden church and a magnificent black and white marble monument was erected to his memory. A translation of part of the Latin inscription on the south side of the canopy runs:

TO CAMPDEN

O fortunate Campden that you possess great riches and the body of your best patron. . . . He has embellished your land with many buildings and flourishing gardens; nor has he allowed the church of God to be neglected, but in his life his devout delight was to help the poor to the utmost. In death grant that he may rest in peace; and may you hold his modest wife, who was the companion of his life, cherish this body well worthy of resurrection, and protect it in your fostering bosom.

Accepting the convention that required the memorials of the wealthy to be fulsome this is not an untrue statement. Sir Baptist Hicks was a good friend and patron to the town. His mansion displayed the extreme Classical fashion of the time, but he had the taste and understanding to build his almshouses in the Cotswold style with just that touch of the seventeenth-century to keep the tradition moving on. One of his minor benefactions was the lantern on his house built to shine out as a guide to travellers benighted on the high lonely wolds above the town. He was Campden's last great lord of the manor.

After Campden House was deliberately fired by the Royalists to whom it had previously given shelter the family did not desert the town. Viscountess Juliana, his eldest daughter, converted the outbuildings left standing after the fire into a residence and lived there for part of her latter years.

It was her steward, William Harrison, who was the principal figure in that strange story known as the Campden Wonder told later in this book. It is said that Edward Harrison, son of the missing and supposedly murdered man, persuaded her to use her influence to have the murderers hanged on Broadway Hill "within sight of Campden" as a warning to possible evil-doers. There was nothing unusual for the period in the granting of such a request, nor does it contradict the general impression one gets from contemporary sources that Lady Juliana was a generous woman, conscious of her duties towards the town and respected and loved by her tenants.

No other large houses were added to Campden's High Street until 1740 when Bedfont House, with a parapet and handsome classical doorway, was built for the Cottrell family by Thomas Woodward, the mason and builder who worked Campden's quarries. It seems likely that he was also responsible for the classical face-lift given to some of Campden's older houses at that time. Looking at them today one realizes that whatever the style of architecture the stone has made all the houses good neighbours.

The Enclosure Act of the parish in 1799 brought greater changes to Campden than it had known since its beginning as a wool market. The great open common fields and unfenced sheep walks around the town now became patterned with miles of drystone walling and this dividing and enclosing the land brought about an enclosing of the classes within definite limits; the old freedom between those who owned land and those who worked it disappeared. Many who had largely depended on common rights of grazing to feed a few animals were obliged to sell their beasts, thus losing that little extra which made all the difference between a tolerable living and bare subsistence. Smaller farmers unable to afford the cost of enclosing their land were obliged to sell it. When the money had gone they were reduced to working for others at a time when a surplus of labour had brought a lowering of wages. Naturally in bad times this increased the ranks of paupers.

Campden had a few small industries such as the silk mills in Sheep Street, a flax mill and a rope and sack works behind the High Street, now remembered by a row of little cottages called Twine Cottages, but by the middle of the century these had been shut down. The clothing trade had passed Campden by because the town did not have the water supply necessary for the making of cloth. It deteriorated as its revenues decreased, the cottages falling into disrepair because their occupants had no means of keeping them in good condition. There was little work except on the land and the wages of farm labourers were so low that there was nothing left after bare necessities had been bought. Campden's population fell as families migrated to the towns in search of better conditions in the new industries.

The Corporation had been practically moribund for many years. It was finally extinguished by the Municipal Corporations Act of 1883 and dissolved in 1886. The days had gone when town and country intermingled and the wool and clothing trade carried on in rural districts played an important part in the country's economy. The making of wealth had now passed to the large industrial cities and little Cotswold towns such as Campden dwindled into insignificance, existing in the past while the big towns seemed to own the present and the future. The image of the backward rustic and the sophisticated town-dweller may have been evident as far back as ancient Greece and Rome but the nineteenth century saw its revival as part of the stock in trade of comedians with just enough truth in the caricature to give it the gloss of reality.

Progress came to Campden as to other places in the form of the penny post, a new Board of Guardians in charge of the Poor Law and Workhouse, the railway and the first resident policeman, but on the whole it stayed self-contained asking little and receiving little from outside. Algernon Gissing, in his *Footpath Way in Gloucestershire* published in 1924, describes a visit he made to the town when a boy. "Here was the old world itself, touched by a magic wand centuries ago and still remaining spellbound." Christopher

Ebrington church near Chipping Campden

Whitfield of a later generation quotes Gissing's statement and adds: "Even then it was an anachronism in a world that turned its power towards the beguilements of an age of industry and mass-production not only of things but of thoughts and ways as well". Christopher Whitfield's *History of Campden* gives a scholarly, detailed and understanding portrait of the town, following Percy Rushen as its painstaking historian.

What was to become of this beautiful anachronism? It was the problem at the beginning of the twentieth century and it is still the problem today. For a while it seemed it might be solved when the Guild of Handicrafts decided to settle in Campden in 1902. This private industrial partnership was inspired and led by C. R. Ashbee, a disciple of William Morris and Ruskin and a passionate idealist, a man best understood by reading his *Craftsmanship in Competitive Industry*, published four years later.

Campden with its continuous tradition of rural craft seemed an ideal home for the Guild. Owing to the agricultural depression the population had fallen and there were many empty cottages and buildings to be let at a low rent because of their poor condition, buildings that could be restored by the Guild workers. Ashbee arranged to rent the old Silk Mills and a number of empty cottages. One hundred and fifty men, women and children including fifty craftsmen came to Campden. The Silk Mill was converted into separate workshops for the various crafts. Braithwaite House near the Woolstapler's Hall was turned into a hostel for single men, the cottages were repaired, and Ashbee restored the Woolstapler's Hall as a dwelling for himself. Two pairs of semi-detached cottages were also built later at Catbrook. The aim of the Guild, "To do good work, and to do it in such a way as to conduce to the welfare of the workman ... to produce honest craftsmanship with or without the aid of machines", was an attempt at practical idealism. In theory it should have succeeded and it is difficult to decide if the project was too early or too late for the times.

Cabinet-making, book-binding, jewellery, work in precious and non-precious metals were some of the crafts practised. There was also a School of Arts and Crafts at Elm Tree House, where lectures were held sponsored by the Oxford University, and summer classes in craftwork based on grants from the local education committees.

6

Snowshill: (above) the Manor (below) dormered cottages

The newcomers were not accepted at first. This was inevitable. From experience with evacuees during the last war many of us know how the sharp cockney tongue, exercised without malice on the difference between town and rural life, can antagonize country folk, though to others the cockneys' characteristic conceit of themselves and their home town has its endearing qualities. But there must have been people in Campden and the surrounding villages to whom the new educational opportunities were a release for the mind and spirit and who benefited greatly by new and exciting contacts with the artists and craftsmen.

When the venture failed financially, caused mainly by the slump of 1905–8 when the goods they made could not be sold and because some of the workers and their families lost faith and idealism when times were bad, a number returned to London. Remembering again the evacuees from town during the last war and their complaints against country life and people and the country people's complaints against them, this becomes easier to understand. In the blood of the country people the fear of the invader throughout the ages bred suspicion and mistrust not easily dispelled, and Campden had been self-contained for so long. One of the benefits of the motoring age has been the breaking down of these intangible barriers.

Finally Mr. Josiah Fels, an American, who had read Ashbee's book and was interested in his theory that craftsmen needed a stake in the country as well as the support of husbandry to provide sustenance during periods of bad trade, bought them a farm of 700 acres in Broad Campden, and a trust was formed for "the encouragement of craftsmanship in conjunction with husbandry with the view to enabling the craftsmen and their families to live a healthier and more reasonable life in the country". Here again was a conception with its origin derived from medieval tradition, a conception practical in itself yet looking to the past for inspiration rather than the future.

It was not a closed community, the twelve remaining guildsmen becoming independent tenants and owners of their own private businesses. It carried on until the 1914–1918 War but soon after the end of the war it came to an end. By 1920 the farm had been sold and the trust closed down. One is forced to the conclusion that the only community working together for the common good which succeeds is one held together by the tight discipline of a religious faith where the will and idiosyncrasies of the individual are ironed out, the kind of life, in fact, the modern craftsman would find intolerable.

Although the experiment failed as far as the Trust was concerned it brought a quiet prosperity to the town and made it known to the outside world as it had not been known for the past three centuries. It attracted men with an interest in the arts, men like F. L. Griggs, R.A. and Paul Woodroffe, who made their homes in Campden. To many others including John Masefield, Ernest Gimson, the Barnsley brothers, Sir Basil Blackwell, Laurence Housman and A. H. Bullen, it became a place to be visited and cherished.

In 1926 a new danger threatened. Dover's Hill, the town's playground since Robert Dover instituted his famous Games, was put up for sale and was offered as a suitable site for a hotel. There was no time to rally supporters and F. L. Griggs bought it, thus gaining time in which to arouse public opinion and secure it as an open place for ever. He was not a wealthy man but he took the risk. An appeal was launched and £2,303 raised against a total of £4,000. Professor C. M. Trevelyan gave the balance and Dover's Hill was conveyed to the National Trust in December 1928. But for the prompt and public-spirited action of Griggs it might have been lost. Few people knew that it was because of his influence and determination that when electricity came to the town in 1928 Campden's famous High Street was not ruined by a network of wires and poles but the electricity was carried behind the town as far as possible and then taken underground. Campden has been fortunate in having men of foresight and understanding to care for its interests when in various crises she might have lost her ancient heritage.

As an outcome of the Campden Society the Campden Trust was formed in 1929 as a small limited company to preserve the architectural beauty of the town. It has done and is still doing good work. One of its achievements was saving the Market Hall, built by Sir Baptist Hicks in 1627, when it was put up for sale: it might have been dismantled and sent to America but for their intervention.

All of Campden's finest and most characteristic buildings are now provisionally scheduled under the Town and Country Planning Act 1957, Section 40, but no Act or Trust can preserve a place if its inhabitants are indifferent to those who would vulgarize it.

Campden, however, is one of those places that has always found devoted lovers to watch over it. To those who knew it in the years between 1920 and 1930 she will always remain in memory as the quiet little grey town whose enchantment we accepted as gratefully and wonderingly as we accepted the unspoilt beauty of the wolds about her. For us age could not wither her for she already belonged to the past, and the past, as Edward Thomas wrote, "is a strange land, most strange. Wind blows not there, nor does rain fall".

If we had been given to looking ahead we might have foreseen that it was impossible for any place to remain in this dream world, but I am glad we did not.

VIII

VILLAGES OF
THE NORTH-WEST CORNER

THE one place in the Cotswolds that everyone has heard about is Broadway, and reactions to it can be violently conflicting. Those who take popular opinion as their guide regard it as the highlight of a Cotswold tour, while your true lover of the region regards its exploitation with sadness, distaste or cynicism according to his character. The best argument put forward by those to whom Broadway has become a place to avoid is that while at the seaside or other centres planned for recreation the tourist trade is legitimate, imposed upon a country village because of its former beauty it is out of keeping with the true function of the place, offending by the shallow and often ludicrous plugging of the past so as to cash in on it. The reply to that argument is another question. What is the true function of any place? Isn't it to provide a decent living for its inhabitants? And why isn't the tourist trade as good as any other for this purpose? Human nature being what it is the two points of view are seldom reconciled.

Some years ago I helped with a private survey of the people who cater for visitors on the Cotswolds and discovered that the majority had come from outside, many from the north of England, to set up as shop-keepers, café proprietors, or to add to retirement incomes by accommodating passing motorists, so that it does not seem that the commercializing of the popular village has been done by those born and bred there. On the other hand the countryman, though he loves his native place and is proud of it, seldom has an eye for the comeliness of his surroundings. A simple illustration was the way any disused quarry, pond or wayside copse was likely to be used for depositing rusty tins, old iron and other squalid litter before there were regular services for rubbish collection. I remember remarking on the beauty of a riot of sweet-williams in his garden to an old man standing by his cottage door. "You'll ne'er get a boiling off 'em," he replied grimly. Perhaps this is not a fair instance for that summer there had been a plague of white butterflies whose caterpillars had probably eaten his cabbages.

Yet Broadway must satisfy a need or people would not flock there in multitudes; and as spending money is one of the pleasures of life today the new Broadway has arisen to satisfy that need. It caters for the wealthy as well as for the more homely parties who come in coaches, and is prettily decked out to please them all.

The village has always been a place of call for travellers, and long before any houses bordered its Broad Way it was on an ancient route between the high wolds and the valley of the Severn passing into Wales. Later, being on the high road to London and travellers being forced to use it, the state of its surface comes frequently into early county records with the usual uncomplimentary descriptions of mire and stones. Habington, the seventeenth-century Worcestershire historian, wrote of "the Vale of Evesham and her foul ways", one of which passed through the village. The coaching era brought it a brief new life and then, as happened at Northleach and Burford, this new trade was extinguished with the coming of the railways and Broadway relapsed into poverty and obscurity. It was during this time that many of its old houses and cottages fell into near ruin.

It had another short revival at the beginning of the twentieth-century when Mary Anderson and other well-known people came to live there. It was during this period that the beauty inherent in the old Cotswold stone buildings began to be recognized, helped by William Morris who always told his love. Old houses were lovingly restored. Those which had degenerated into labourers' tenements, or in one instance the village lock-up and workhouse, became the homes of artists and craftsmen escaping from the grime and ugliness of the Industrial Revolution and seeking new inspiration from the countryside. The reputation thus gained as one of the most beautiful villages on the Cotswolds has persisted to this day.

But this was a revival imposed upon it by outsiders and like most revivals it died when its founders died and as the back-to-the-country movement faded away. The heart had gone out of Broadway and its continuity broken beyond repair in the bad days of the nineteenth century, and no amount of cosseting from people whose main interests were in London could resuscitate it. Its new development was as a show village, which must have puzzled the old Cotsallers to whom "Broddy" was a village like any other only with more pubs and a longer hill to climb for anyone wanting to get out of it.

But there is one part of Broadway, aloof from the souvenir shops and hotels, existing still in its own quiet world. About a mile along the elm-shaded road to Snowshill is the old church, dedicated to St. Aedburg, granddaughter of King Alfred. After years of neglect it has now been renovated and restored, although the modern church, called by Algernon Gissing "an architecturally unhappy structure" has long taken its place as the parish church, chiefly because it is nearer the main part of the village.

The old church is not forgotten or entirely neglected. There were jars of fresh tall tulips lighting up the interior when I saw it last spring, and the churchyard, beautiful with its great sycamore, holly and yew trees and enclosed on one side by a tall clipped yew hedge of the adjoining manor-house, was well-kept, the grass newly mown and fresh flowers on some of the old graves. In its quiet green leafy hollow with a stream running just below the churchyard it is a bird-haunted place. As I sat on the worn stone steps leading up and over the churchyard wall a thrush sang from the sycamore, cuckoos called from beyond the stream, a jay slipped quietly into the trees without his usual warning screech, tits went busily in and out of holes in the churchyard wall, jackdaws circled the sturdy square tower as they must have done for centuries, while a blackbird poked the turf fiercely for worms to feed his family, for I watched him fly off with his beak so full that the food dangled on each side of his face like a monstrous drooping moustache.

On the east wall of the chancel is a small brass to Anthony Daston, sheriff of the county and lord of the manor in Elizabethan times. He wears a breastplate and a skirt of mail, and carries a long sword at his side. "A playne stone with a cros graduted over hym and his wydowe, the most bountifull gentilwoman for hospitality of her degree in England Mistres Daston of Broadweye" which Habington records as being under the effigy has disappeared, also a memorial brass to William Sheldon and Ciceley his wife. Anne

Daston was a Sheldon by birth, and the Sheldon's were Broadway's last great land-owning family.

Court House, beside the church, is on the site of the manor house, of which only the gateway remains of the original building. The stone of the later house has now mellowed and holds itself with true Cotswold grace and reserve. Lawns and flower beds and a great yew hedge between it and the churchyard make yet another of those felicitous groupings that are one of Cotswold's attractions.

At the lower end of the village towards the Vale of Evesham a considerable number of new dwellings have been erected in recent years. These are the kind of small houses and bungalows one finds on the outskirts of any town, pleasant and bright but of no architectural distinction. In the designing of its modern dwellings Broadway has turned its back on the Cotswold tradition and goes towards the valley. There are occasions when I feel this is a more honest if less interesting form of progress than the plugging of a picturesque antiquity which has lost all reality.

After leaving Broadway's old church one comes to Snowshill in about a mile and a half, the road climbing all the way and becoming steeper as it approaches the village. This was an old coach road and the horses must have found it a hard pull to the uplands. Snowshill's position out on the wolds well behind the escarpment promises wide views in all directions, particularly towards Worcestershire. It is these unfoldings of land and sky which make the hill country so memorable. Mile after mile of pastures and cornfields in the foreground, long wooded crests with other hilltops patterned in every shade of green, and slopes beyond, some dark with trees, others growing dim and misty blue on the horizon, with glimpses of church towers, the huddled roofs of villages, and patches of dense woodland emphasizing the paler tones of corn and grass and plough.

It is for these wide prospects and for its situation once so isolated on the open wolds, that the name of Snowshill is cherished by those who love walking the Cotswold hills or who did so in their youth. On every side are old tracks and paths reaching to the innermost and outermost corners of the region, to the villages of Stanton and Stanway, named after the stone which made them, to Laverton and Buckland in their lower green wooded valley.

The village consists of little more than a few old cottages, a large gabled stone house with open terraced gardens, a beautifully preserved seventeenth-century manor house once the home of the Sambach family, but now looked after by the National Trust.

The tiny church of St. Barnabas on the green was entirely re-built in 1864 and a fifteenth-century font and a Jacobean pulpit are all that remains of the old church. Its predecessor was also small, consisting of a nave and west tower with battlements and pinnacles. It was still in use when Dr. Parsons, Chancellor of the Diocese of Gloucester, made his notes on the parish churches of Stanton and Snowshill about 1710.

Dr. Parson's *A Parochial Visitation of the County of Gloucestershire* is one of the best sources we have for details about the Cotswold churches in his time. As well as being interested in ecclesiastical architecture he also had a historian's curiosity about the general aspect of the villages he visited, their boundaries, the kind of soil, the crops grown and such details and recorded his findings. In the Bodleian Library along with his manuscript notes is a short sum-mary of his life and work written by Dr. Rawlinson with a con-cluding paragraph showing that the reverend doctors of that day were as prone to spiteful criticism of their contemporaries as the learned doctors of our own times. It runs: "He made the following collection towards the History and Antiquities of Gloster, of which some, though little use was made in that pompous but injudicious piece published by Sir Robert Atkyns, of Sapperton, in that county." A scathing remark to make about Sir Robert's *History of Gloucestershire* soon to become the standard work of the county.

Between the years 1710 and the end of the century the little Norman church at Snowshill must have fallen into ruin. If it could have been preserved it would have made the focal point lacking to give it the true unity of an upland village. As it is, with the old cottages turning their backs to the green in grey reserve, the manor house screened by a wall on one side of the triangle, the village seems to be holding itself aloof, and though the buildings are not scattered they look outward rather than inward. As a community, however, it has always been well-knit, a legacy from the days when its position isolated it in bad weather and co-operation between the villagers was necessary if life was to be tolerated when they were cut off from the outside world.

According to Ogilby's road-book of 1675 one of the four main roads passing through Gloucestershire went through Snowshill. Starting at Gloucester its route was Cheltenham, Winchcombe, Stanway, Snowshill, Chipping Campden, leaving the county at Mickleton to finish at Stratford-on-Avon. It can still be followed and for those who like walking high lonely roads the two and a half miles or so from Snowshill to Springhill where it crosses the Five Mile Drive at its highest point is one of the finest upland walks I know.

About a mile out of the village it crosses Buckle Street, a cross-roads of great antiquity, and then comes to Seven Wells, once a stopping place for coaches but now a quiet group of farm buildings. On the opposite side of the Five Mile Drive the road begins a slow descent to the Westington end of Campden, broad and tree-shaded for part of the way and still keeping an air of antiquity despite its change into a main road.

One of the first sewing machines was invented at Snowshill by Charles Keyte in 1842. His machine is now in the Science Museum at South Kensington, and looks a strange contraption to our eyes with its heavy wooden stool and wheel, but without Keyte's invention the sewing machine as we know it today might have taken longer to evolve.

Some years ago wishing to discover if he had any honour in his own village I asked several people but none had heard of it, though the family was well-known as belonging to Campden and the vicinity. Percy Rushen's massive history of Campden records many members of the family from the early seventeenth century onward including one who gave a treble bell to Campden church inscribed, "Captain Thomas Keyte gave me, ledar of this ring, 1683;" "Jno. Keyte wheelwright in 1708", and another Thomas who was a smith. A Mary Keyte was married to a Hulls, a family also interested in mechanical devices. Jonathan Hull is a name still known to many marine engineers because of the steam tug he invented. A working model he built was unsuccessful, for which he was not to blame, and its failure provoked the following skit. The "paper skull" refers to the paper cap worn by Hull as by all mechanics at that time.

Jonathan Hull
With his paper skull,
Tried to make a machine
To go against wind and stream;
But he, like an ass
Couldn't bring it to pass
So at last was ashamed to be seen.

This doggerel typifies the rustic attitude to genius in their midst and shows one of the less pleasing aspects of rural life when it is cut off from the outside world. A broader outlook is one of the benefits brought by the migrants from the towns who are slowly taking over the villages today.

Buckland lies less than a mile across the fields from Laverton. The dark wooded shoulder of Burhill here juts out into the plain sheltering the village from the north. Withdrawn amongst orchards and gardens it is a village with a cherished look. In 1714 a house in Buckland became the home of the Granvilles, who lived there temporarily as political refugees when George I came to the throne. Mary Granville, afterwards Mrs. Delany, and described by Edmund Burke as "the highest-bred woman in the world and the woman of fashion of all ages" was about sixteen when she came to Buckland from Whitehall where she had lived with her uncle, Sir John Stanley, secretary to the Duke of Shrewsbury. Accustomed to the elegancies and sophistication of the court, country life at first seemed tedious because of the lack of congenial companions. Her acquaintance with Sally Kirkham, daughter of the rector of Stanton was frowned on because Sally was something of a tomboy, and this opposition gave a romantic spur to the friendship.

"We met in the fields as often as we had opportunity," wrote Mrs. Delany in her *Memoirs*, calling up a picture of two high-spirited girls meeting secretly and probably giggling a little at the way they had defeated their elders as they walked embraced in the quiet lanes discussing life with earnestness as well as laughter as young people will.

Mary Granville grew to love the village. "Nothing could be more fragrant and rural; the sheep and cows come bleating and lowing to the pales of the garden. At some distance on the left hand was a rookery, on the right a little clear brook runs winding

through a copse of young elms . . ." is the nostalgic description
she wrote years after. And though this pastoral scene has known
many changes since then there are times in Buckland when one
can easily imagine oneself back in those days.

Its church of St. Michael fortunately escaped the nineteenth-
century restorers, perhaps because it was not allowed to deteriorate
like so many village churches in the eighteenth century. This was
the period when the young John Wesley preached here, when
there was much coming and going between the Kirkham family
of Stanton, the Granvilles and Tookers of Buckland, the Winningtons and Griffiths of Broadway, all having some connection with
the church, and with wider interests than the day-to-day gossip
of the countryside.

Mr. Tooker, rector of Buckland from 1714 to 1747, nicknamed
Tranio by the younger members of the group, was a man of
Jacobite sympathies. He was also one of those clerical "characters"
for which the eighteenth century was renowned. Mrs. Delany
describes him as having "a sort of droll wit and repartee that was
diverting, but would have been more so, had it not been somewhat out of character and unbecoming to the dignity of his
profession".

Be that as it may he had the understanding to preserve the
smaller treasures of his church, the fifteenth-century glass, the
sixteenth-century benches and panelling, the Buckland Bowl of
maplewood with the tiny silver disc engraved most delicately
with a picture of St. Margaret on the base inside, the velvet pall
embroidered in gold, silver and coloured silks made out of ancient
vestments by an accomplished needlewoman of the fifteenth
century, embroidery of the kind which made England famous
throughout Europe for the beauty of its workmanship and design.
He also made no permanent alterations to the rectory built by
a former rector, William Grafton, with its hall reaching to the
roof timbers and in one of the tall windows a rebus showing a tun
with the graft of a tree rising out of it.

Stanton, a little more than a mile south, is the largest village of
the three. As well as the upland road from Snowshill and the
footpaths from Buckland and Laverton it can be reached from the
Vale. Chestnut, oak and elm trees line the valley approach so that
coming to it for the first time one is surprised to see it open out as

an upland village. The name in its Anglo-Saxon form means a settlement where stone is quarried and suits it well.

Most of its houses were built in the early seventeenth century at the time when the Cotswold building tradition was at its best, as can be seen from the dates, 1604, 1615 and 1618 carved on them. It was a period when the yeoman farmers of the district reached the peak of their prosperity, and the houses reflect between them every possible variation within the Cotswold vernacular that the stone masons could devise.

Of the houses before this date Warren House, built by Thomas Warren of Snowshill in 1577, has Tudor roses and fleurs-de-lis on a beautiful plaster ceiling, and was once known as the manor house. The history of Stanton Court, a handsome Elizabethan mansion, is more involved, but it was the Izod family, well known around Campden and Broadway, and afterwards the Wynniatts, who were responsible for many of the earlier additions and alterations.

The family, however, one associates with Stanton in the early eighteenth century is the Kirkhams, whose name one finds repeatedly in Mrs. Delany's *Memoirs* and the Journals of John Wesley and other lesser known chronicles of those days which have come down to us. On the north wall of the chancel of the parish church is a mural tablet which reads:

Near this place
are interr'd the Bodies of
Lionel and Robert, Son and Grandson of
Henry Kirkham, all successively Rectors of this Parish
As also of
Henrietta Kirkham and Penelope
Wife of Tho. Woods, Clerk
Daughter of the above-named Henry
Thomas Woods the son of Penelope
Sarah ye Wife of John Chapone, Clerk
and daughter of Lionel above-mentioned
Mary the wife of Robert Kirkham
and Three of their Daughters
Who died in their Infancy
To whose Memory this monument was erected in
Year of our Lord
MDCCLXVII

Sarah Kirkham, whose appearance "of being too free and masculine" displeased Mary Granville's father, though when he knew her better he admitted her "extraordinary understanding, lively imagination and humane disposition", was the one whose influence was the most pervasive, though she lived out her life in a quiet county district happy with a modest home and family. That she was a woman of character and understanding is shown not only in the constant references to her in John Wesley's Journals and Mrs. Delany's *Memoirs* and letters but in the way she helped Elizabeth Elstob, the Anglo-Saxon scholar, author of *Anglo-Saxon Homilies*.

Sarah was introduced to her by George Ballard, the antiquary of Chipping Campden, another Anglo-Saxon scholar who compiled his own Anglo-Saxon dictionary while working as a stay and habit maker to help support his widowed mother. Elizabeth Elstob was working as a schoolmistress in Evesham and studying hard in her spare time, which, according to letters she wrote to Ballard, was very meagre. Sally realized the value of Elizabeth Elstob's studies and was compassionately aware that her occupation gave her little time for private study. She wrote to Mary Granville who had married Mr. Pendarves, her first husband, and was living in London. Through her influence at Court Mary Pendarves managed to bring the letter to the notice of Queen Caroline, reporting later that the queen had said she "never in her life read a better letter, and ordered immediately a hundred pounds for Mrs. Elstob".

John Wesley became acquainted with the Kirkhams through his friend, Robin Griffiths, a New College man, whose father was vicar of Broadway. In *The Young Mr. Wesley* by V. H. H. Green, there is a chapter "The Cotswold Scene" giving an idyllic picture of the way the younger members of this cultivated group, the Granvilles, Griffiths, Kirkhams, the Winningtons and Mr. Izod employed themselves. They gave one another nicknames as was the fashion of the times. Wesley was Cyrus, Mary Granville Aspasia, Sarah Kirkham Varanese, Anne Granville Selima, and so on. Riding, walking, singing, dancing, a little mild flirtation as well as serious discussion about religion and the problems of the day occupied their time. And how the talk flowed between them! It might be summed up in a remark in a letter from Sally to

Elizabeth Elstob some years later. "Conversation is the proper entertainment of a thinking person," she wrote.

John Wesley's entrance into this lively group must have influenced him greatly and it is significant that he turned more naturally to its feminine members. He was more at ease with young women, having been brought up with sisters who sought his counsel and looked up to him. It must have been the happiest and less inhibited period of his life, an opening out of a freer and more refined social world than he had known at home; it certainly helped to counteract the gauche mannerisms due to his dour upbringing.

There is no doubt that Sally Kirkham with her wit and lively imagination played a great part in it. It was inevitable he should fall in love with her, but marriage between them was impossible. He was only recently ordained, still in debt, with a family who had no wealthy connections to help him; and advancement depended chiefly on patronage in those days.

Sally married John Chapone and Wesley was at the wedding. "May God give her the happiness she deserves," he wrote in his diary. Sally was happy in her husband and her five children, but the affection between them remained. If Wesley was deeply stricken by her loss he made no outward sign and would not admit it even to himself. In any case his religion and high principles would have prevented him making any show of it, or it may have been that only in after years did he become fully aware of his dependence upon her understanding. Mr. Green suggests that a shrinking from physical intimacy was part of his make-up and in the light of what we know of his later life I think Mr. Green's theory is the right one. This distaste showed itself more plainly as he grew older. On many occasions in public as well as privately he uttered warnings about the temptations lurking in the love of women, and a longing "to attain such a purity of thought as suits a candidate for that state wherein they neither marry nor are given in marriage, but are as angels of God in Heaven."

His marriage later to Molly Vazielle was an unhappy one. Mr. Green makes out a strong case for Wesley's emotional immaturity. Indeed when one remembers how he was surrounded by the lively affectionate young women of Stanton and Buckland, with innumerable opportunities for long private talks and walks it is a wonder how he escaped marriage with one of them except by his own reluctance to take the step. Men with poorer prospects than his persuaded young women or their parents that their position could easily improve with the years, and there is no evidence at all that he was not wholly welcomed by the elders without regard for his material prosperity.

After the middle of the eighteenth century there are few records from outside sources concerning Stanton. The young people who had shared their country pastimes with John Wesley, who had listened to him preach in Buckland, Stanton and Broadway and discussed his sermons afterwards were either married or left the district. Stanton's brief golden age was over.

By the end of the nineteenth century the village was suffering from the paralysis affecting most rural areas at that period. In 1874 the chancel of the church was rebuilt; in 1896 Miss Elizabeth Mills of Warren House left money for more restoration which was carried out under the supervision of Sir Arthur Bloomfield, so that even the church where the Kirkhams had been rectors for so many years was changed.

But as has happened before on Cotswold the village was saved from the less pleasing makeshifts of the early twentieth century by a newcomer from the north, Philip Stott, of Oldham, afterwards Sir Philip Stott. He fell in love with it, purchasing the greater part, and set about repairing and restoring the old houses and cottages. There was some delay owing to the difficulties of getting supplies and labour during the 1914–1918 War, but eventually he turned it into one of the most comely villages on the Cotswolds, and one for which he provided practical amenities as well, a water supply, electric light, a cricket pitch and a swimming pool.

A list of the work he did and his benefactions to Stanton are given in Mr. E. A. B. Barnard's book *Stanton and Snowshill*, published by the University Press in 1927. This is a scholarly history of the two villages and one which has led the way throughout the country to a more conscientious study of local history through the medium of parish registers and other official documents.

An upland scene

IX

THE WINDRUSH

THE Windrush is the largest of the Cotswold rivers, and from its source to Newbridge in Oxfordshire where it flows into the Thames it covers some thirty miles.

The head valley is just south of Snowshill, a waterless valley except in seasons of heavy rain. One has to come two miles south to Cutsdean to find the first bubbling spring in a small hollow, and this in summer is often reduced to a muddy patch where butterflies spread their wings on the sun-baked earth and bees seek the tiny waterdrops at the feet of the tattered clumps of rushes. Just beyond Ford a mile or so on there is sufficient water for the beginning of an insignificant stream. This small beginning, however, is a place where birds gather, the water bringing them down from the high dry wolds to drink and bathe; in springtime one could trace the stream by the band of bird-song along its banks, blackbirds, thrushes, finches, twittering swallows and martins and the plaintive willow wren.

Cutsdean is a hillside village 750 feet up, with enormous stone barns and its houses and cottages spread out on the west slope of the hill. It belonged to Worcestershire for over a thousand years and is shown as an enclave on the oldest maps where even the roads are absent. The question of how Worcestershire could claim such a typical Cotswold parish is answered, of course, in the complicated history of ecclesiastical holdings of separate manors which came to the church in its early days as gifts from kings and nobles or were bought by wealthy churchmen before the shires were defined as such. Cutsdean was an estate of a Bishop of Worcester who transferred it to his own shire because of the valuable upland sheep pastures. In 1931 it was taken into Gloucestershire officially, but it has always belonged to the county in spirit and is as typical a piece of Cotswold to be found in the whole region.

By the time the Windrush has wound a mile or so south to

Guiting Power: restored cottages on the village green

Temple Guiting it has become a recognizable stream at all times of the year. Temple Guiting's name comes from the military order of Templars who had a small preceptory there in the twelfth century. There are records showing that it was the Templars who in 1182 harnessed the stream to work two fulling mills, one at Kineton and another at Barton, two hamlets between Temple Guiting and Guiting Power. One would like to think that the little stone-slab bridge at Kineton also belonged to the twelfth century, for its stones are worn with the passing of many feet. There is nothing to be seen of the mills today, though the foundations might be discovered by careful excavation. The river here has scoured itself a deep gorge into the valley.

The most ancient house, once the summer residence of the Bishop of Oxford and an almost perfect example of Tudor architecture, is in the park at Temple Guiting. It has a pigeon house built into one wall of the house while a cupola above the roof gave the birds their own entrance. Smoke-blackened rafters in the attics show that it once possessed a great hall rising to the full height of the building.

When the Windrush comes to the more open valley holding the straggling village of Naunton on its banks it has been fed by two small tributaries, one coming from Guiting Wood and another flowing along the narrow grassy valley dotted with willows and poplars leading to Guiting Power. This village at the junction of the two streams with its cottages standing haphazard fashion on the slopes above the river as well as along the road is one of those examples of how humble cottages of Cotswold stone however simple in design, fit into the landscape and are absorbed by it.

All that remains to remind us of the original Guiting Grange, a dependency of Bruern Abbey in Oxfordshire, are the field names. One "Bier Way Piece" could have received its name because traces of a chapel in a field near the modern Guiting Grange may have been a mortuary, and the funeral processions passed across the field on its way to the burial.

The Windrush, keeping to the right side of the valley with open meadows on the left and steep slopes, some of them wooded, on the right, comes to Naunton. The church is perched on the left bank and was considerably restored in 1878, a date which speaks for itself. The houses keep close to the stream for nearly a mile, the road separated from the water by narrow green water-meadows. The best way to see the village is to look at it over a low stone wall on the Stow road about half way between Harford Bridge and the Fox Inn at Guiting Power. Here the village and the river winding between rushy banks can be seen as a complete picture against a background of hillside topped with the ridge skyline, the ridge which carries the prehistoric ridgeway on its way to Stow. Seeing Naunton from this point it becomes evident that despite the fact it lies in green water-meadows it is an upland village. From this point, also, one can see the ancient dove-cot standing alone in a field. The four gables, steeply pitched, have a small window in each face, and there is a string moulding sharply undercut below the gables, a feature which kept the rats from climbing up into the holes.

Meandering in lazy coils the river runs south-easterly past Aston Farm and another mill to flow under Harford Bridge and soon leaves the limestone behind for the clays of Bourton Vale. Beyond Bourton on the Water it is joined by the Dikler coming down from the north, and on a raised bed of gravel midway between the two rivers there was once a small late Bronze Age settlement. Later on, in the Iron Age, an area of fifty-six acres was enclosed by double ramparts and ditches. Traces of circular wattle and daub huts roofed with thatch have been found suggesting a crowded population within the earthern banks. It would appear to have been inhabited both before and after the Belgic invasion and to have been deserted only when the Foss Way and a Roman posting station on the road near where Bourton Bridge now stands were made. It was occupied again after the Romans left and the last people to live there were the Saxons who took over the remains of the Romano-British huts. It was the Saxons who christened the place Salmonsbury or "Ploughman's encampment" and it bears this name in a charter of 779 by Offa, King of Mercia.

Among the many finds when the earthworks were excavated just before the last great war were iron bars, about thirty inches long, made of ore probably from the Forest of Dean, and a Saxon weaver's hut said to be one of the most perfect to be uncovered in England. There is a delightful model of it in the British Museum. Salmonsbury finally became the meeting place of the hundred which includes Bourton. Today the only visible evidence of its past history is a much decayed eastern rampart.

Where the Windrush meets the Foss Way some three miles south-west of Stow a road turns east to Bourton on the Water, and then road and river keep together for a quarter of a mile, the pollard willows on the river banks going with them to the outskirts of the town, when the river disappears behind the houses fronting the road. It is seen again in the centre of the town neatly channelled and margined by green lawns and willows and crossed by a series of little bridges making a charming little promenade to enchant its many visitors.

Using the river to enhance the town centre has paid good dividends though I doubt if this was the original intention. It seems more likely that it grew naturally out of the position of the road and river and houses and was then formalized into its present delightful aspect by someone with a good sense of landscape planning. Apart from this centre Bourton on the Water seems to consist mainly of the kind of houses one finds on the outskirts of any town, beginning with the early Victorian villas and graduating to the newest bungalows on the outermost fringes. The ancient manor house has long since been destroyed, but there is one Cotswold building with sun-dials dated 1689 near the Victoria Hall, and in Moore Road some good modern stone houses following the Cotswold tradition. Apart from these only the river comes from the hills.

For children and those who still enjoy miniature toys there is the model village, a most ingenious piece of work and lovingly put together. It also makes somewhere for the visitors to go and is a great asset to the town.

On occasions I have wondered why so many people are attracted to Bourton and why its fame has spread so widely. I put the question to a stout elderly lady from Lancashire who was contemplating the ducks on the water with a bemused satisfaction, and being conditioned by television to the questioning of inquisitive strangers she was as pleased to talk to me as I was to talk to her.

"I go for the ride, love, and it rests me legs. As long as I find a good cup of tea and a shutter at t'other end I don't mind where I go, if I'm welcome, that is," she added shrewdly.

She took a good lick all round the ice-cream sandwich she was holding to show me what she meant, and I felt suddenly ashamed I had asked the question. Any place which gives pleasure to its visitors justifies itself, and as one café proprietor discussing the summer trade said to me: "We don't ask 'em to come. They just do. And come back again."

"Isn't there a little arrangement with the coach people?" I asked tentatively.

He smiled. "I'm in this for business not my health, but all the same they wouldn't come if they didn't want to."

Nearly four miles downstream the Windrush is joined by the Sherborne Brooke coming from the north, and after passing Wiers Mill it continues its meanderings in a series of loops past Windrush village and Little Barrington on one side and Great Barrington and Taynton on the other to come to Burford.

Because it takes its name from the river one would expect the river to play an important part in the Windrush village make-up, but the church and houses lie above the valley and to reach the river bank one must take a track leading off the road to the weir and mill. The church of St. Peter, on the top of a sloping green shaded by lime trees is the focal point of the village.

Despite the loss of its two porches and the severe restoration of 1874 it makes a very pleasant picture perched high with the old stone mounting block by the churchyard gate as it was in the days when the horse not the motor car was the chief means of transport. The south doorway is one of the most fascinating on the Cots-wolds, and this in a region where almost every church can show a good example of Norman work. A double row of beakheads, each one different, continues down the jambs as well as along the arch, the carving as bold and vigorous today as when it was first exe-cuted. Six slanting shafts and capitals of the chancel arch show all the traditional Norman patterns, spiral flutings, dog-tooth, chevron and lozenge designs.

A solitary stone ram's head, the only carving to adorn the plain Transitional arcading, stands out where one arch begins to spring from its pillar, as if put there as a symbol of the good sheep country surrounding the village. Corbel heads of the kingpost frames of the roof have the true spirit of the grotesque, and a Jacobean pulpit carries on the good work with a patterning of roses and dragons.

In the churchyard tombs and tombstones are huddled together with scarce an inch between them, for the slope of the hillside provides only a small flat area surrounding the church. All have the good lettering of the early eighteenth century, but some of the box tombs are so loaded with ornament that they give the impression the stone masons' pleasure in the work had run away with them. A few have the heavy corded sausage-like shapes on large table-tops and are finished at the sides not only with the typical shell patterns but with centre motifs depicting the heads of sheep instead of the usual cherubs, the horns most ingeniously continuing the lines of the fluted shell edges. Whoever had designed them clearly wished to show that the tombs were made for men connected with wool and sheep, and had adapted the designs accordingly.

Looking closely at the memorials in each Cotswold churchyard one soon begins to distinguish within the convention of the period small differences in each locality, the mark of individual craftsmen or families of craftsmen who served it, as well as to notice how the tradition was carried over from one generation to another. In her book *Cotswold Stone* Freda Derrick finishes one of the chapters with the following words and a visit to any churchyard will point her conclusions.

"It was in decorating the Cotswold churches that the men who worked the oolite had learned to be artists in stone. It was in the Cotswold churchyards that they made a last stand together as decorative craftsmen."

Little Barrington, on the south side of the river, is set back the width of a narrow road around the rim of a large hollow, once a quarry but now a grass-grown bowl with a broken open end. Pollarded elms are also set about the rim providing a dappled shade and a changing decoration of rounded leafage and bare twiggery to this simple picture. At the foot of the bowl a spring gushes out of the rock to make a ribbon of brighter green as the overflow from the stone trough trickles across the grass to where it is channelled at the bottom of a cottage garden, after which it crosses a field to join a branch of the Windrush on the edge of Barrington Park. For centuries this spring was the village water supply, and the flat bottom of the hollow is worn by narrow paths made by the inhabitants fetching their water. Each cottage on the lip of the hollow has its own variation in the Cotswold style; one has an enclosed gothic porch, another a tiny dormer, another a plain flat front and so on. It is the grouping of the whole which makes the picture a satisfying one.

This is a good stone country. Not only the cottages of the two Barrington villages came from the local quarries but their two churches and the mansion of Barrington Park as well. Little Barrington's church is some distance from the village in a shallow dip on the hill-top. It is long, low and narrow with a squat tower at the west end and a tiny sanctus bell-cote at the east of the nave, and it gives the impression of crouching down out of the rough winds of the open wolds around it. It is a homely little church with a homely grassy churchyard containing no imposing monuments to great or important people. Lichened tombstones lean in all directions shaded by ancient yews and two conifers whose ragged tops are ravaged by the perpetual wind.

I last saw it one grey February day. The churchyard was dotted with clumps of snowdrops in full flower which endured the gusty showers without apparent hurt. It was the kind of day when an isolated old church is a sad grey place. A touch of poignancy was added to the melancholy by the stone floor hollowed in places by the wear of many years, the only visible remembrance of the many who had once worshipped here.

From Little Barrington one can continue to Burford in sight of the river nearly all the way on a narrow road enclosed by low stone walls which rise and fall gently with the contours of the slopes. The river is open here, the willows and other riverside trees well spaced out, and this "soft surrounding scene" as Tom Moore described Barrington Park in one of his verses, describes the whole of this gentle stretch of the river.

On the opposite side lies the village of Great Barrington, the great deer park and the late Renaissance mansion built by Charles Talbot, Lord Chancellor in the reign of George II. Part of Great Barrington was in Berkshire until 1844, when it was transferred to Gloucestershire. This would be easier to understand if it had once belonged to Oxfordshire for in less than two miles after leaving Great Barrington the border is reached and the Windrush comes into that county.

At Taynton, the next village on the river, thatch takes the place of stone slates on some of the cottage roofs, and their gardens in the flowering season are as beautiful as any I know, roses rioting to the roof and falls of brilliantly-coloured plants luxuriating over the stone walls. It has one farm and group of farm buildings, however, that are the Cotswold vernacular at its best. Taynton was famous in the Middle Ages for its quarries. The stone was not only used locally but was taken to Oxford and London by water for the building of colleges, churches, houses and barns. Christopher Wren knew it well. The quarries lie north of the village and beyond them are the equally famous quarries of Milton. One of the characteristics of the stone is its fine yellow colour, more golden than the orange yellow of the oolite in other Cotswold districts.

The Windrush comes into Burford at the oldest part of the town where a low-arched bridge makes a charming beginning to the long wide main street that rises slowly to the hill-top. Domesday records a small settlement by the river such as would naturally grow up about a ford which was the crossing place of an ancient direct route coming from the north Cotswolds to the upper crossing of the Thames. There is evidence that the original bridge was built well before 1322, for at that time according to the Burford Records it was in a ruinous condition and the following year pontage for a period of three years was granted for its repair. Since then it has been repaired and altered many times, but the weathering of the stone soon achieves a harmony with its more ancient parts and restoration after a tank broke down the parapet during the last war is now barely noticeable.

Although Burford is in Oxfordshire she has not left the Cotswolds. To a sensitive observer, however, despite the temporary accretions of the tourist-catching trade covering so many picturesque places with a veneer of sameness, the influence of the ancient Forest of Wychwood can still be felt.

Burford does not wear her antiquity too gravely; it has undergone too many changes for that to be possible. To see it at its best one needs a sparkling day and then it can look enchanting from whichever position one chooses. I can never decide whether I prefer the view up the main street from the bridge where the border of pollarded limes seems to be marching with the road or looking down on it from the Witney-Northleach highway at the top of the hill and so bringing in a backcloth of hills beyond the old bridge. The first moment of vision is the best. Among the vistas and hidden corners are many architectural delights and puzzles. The solution to some of the puzzles can be found by looking at the backs of the buildings which have remained comparatively unchanged while the fronts have been altered to suit the passing fashions of the years. Although the purist might be shocked the general effect is lively and pleasing. One also senses a sturdiness which no amount of arti-craftiness can conceal.

To embark on a history of the town would be foolish when it has been written in detail with scholarship, urbanity and true appreciation of its parts by Mrs. Gretton in her book *Burford*. Moreover she did not come from outside to write it. It was her home and she knew it intimately, watching through the years as one watches the face of a beloved. With the instinct of the true historian she was conscious all the time of what had gone before and how and why the political and economic issues of each decade wrought fresh changes. Looking for evidence of the past in old documents she translated her findings into terms of human existence and any writer of local history could take her book as a pattern.

The fabric of the church began as a simple nave, tower and chancel in the early twelfth century. The main reconstructions came in the late fourteenth and fifteenth centuries. The Chapel of the Gild Marchants of Burford, once a separate building, was altered so as to join on to the porch and the south aisle, and later on the old Gild Chapel became known as the Sylvester Aisle from the memorials to that family on its south wall.

There are some magnificent tombs in the churchyards with strange bolster-like tops which some say represent corded woolbales and others the iron hearse placed over a coffin at a funeral to carry the pall. They are decorated with Renaissance ornament, heavy swags, fruit and smiling fat cherubs sprouting inadequate wings or with funereal symbols of death, skulls, bones and hourglasses, but all are solid, dignified and so heavy as to look immovable. Because of the moist airs of the river the stone is unusually dark under the accretions of orange and silver lichen and bosses of green moss.

When the men of Burford, who were great poachers, went

hunting in the Forest of Wychwood it is said that the venison was hidden in these tombs until it could be safely cleared. One hears the same stories about box tombs from other counties as well, particularly about churchyards on smugglers' routes where they became depositories for brandy and lace, or venison when near a great forest as at Burford. Evidently the only people who were not in the secret were the Excise men and game wardens.

The collection of memorials inside the church are of every possible kind from the fifteenth-century brasses of John Spycer and his wife Alys to the great Tanfield monument overshadowing all the others rather like the family overshadowed the town when they were alive. It was erected by Lady Tanfield in 1628 in honour of her husband Lord Chief Justice Sir Lawrence Tanfield, and is an elaborate show of grief for a man the town hated and who still takes up far too much room in the church. The inscription tells us it is in memory of "his virtues and her sorrows". History speaks of him as "corrupt and avaricious in public life, grasping and overbearing as a landlord". He was the first cause of Burford's loss of civic liberties, according to Mrs. Gretton, for when he bought the old Burford Priory and became lord of the manor he set about reducing the Corporation's rights and powers by the weight of his authority and none of the citizens had the moral strength or knowledge of the law to oppose him.

He built a handsome mansion on the site of the old priory and it was Burford's tragedy that instead of a man who would have helped them to prosperity like Sir Baptist Hicks at Campden they were ruled by one who cared only for his own aggrandisement. His wife, a Norfolk woman, was equally disliked, particularly at Great Tew where her husband was also lord of the manor and where the villagers complained: "She saith that we are more worthy to be ground to powder than to have any favour showed to us, and that she will play the very devil among us". Yet though she was as ruthless as her husband, never seeking to mitigate the lot of those under his hard rule, the verses on the grandiose tomb have a piteous quality.

> Love made me a Poet
> And this I writt
> My harte did do y't
> And not my witt.

The story of Elizabeth Tanfield, their only child, is a sad one. They had no joy of her and she certainly had no joy in being their daughter. Tanfield may have been disappointed in not having a male heir to inherit his new mansion and perhaps this was the cause of his harshness to her. Married at fifteen to Henry Carey, Viscount Falkland, a rake and a spendthrift, and soon neglected by him she turned for comfort to the church of Rome. For this her father disinherited her, her son Lucius being taken away from her when he was a child and brought up as his grandfather's heir. At one time she was in actual want, but when Lucius Carey inherited his grandfather's estate he looked after her. She employed her lonely hours writing hymns, the lives of several saints and translating the works of Cardinal Perron, and one can only hope this brought her peace and comfort. It seems likely that her son inherited his love of scholarship and literary tendencies from her. All accounts show him to have been a sensitive and charming man, totally unlike his spendthrift father and overbearing grandfather.

Lucius's wife is represented on the Tanfield tomb by the bust of a pretty golden-haired woman. His father quarrelled with him for marrying a woman without a dowry but two years after the marriage Lord Falkland died from a riding accident. The title was all Lucius Carey inherited; to pay his father's debts he sold Burford Priory for £7,000 to William Lenthall, Speaker of the House of Commons in the Long Parliament, and retired to Great Tew, also left to him by his grandfather Judge Tanfield.

Here he led the quiet scholarly life he preferred. According to Lord Clarendon, "his house . . . looked like a university itself by the company always found there . . . and indeed all men of eminent parts and faculties in Oxford . . . beside those who resolved thither from London . . ." Many of the important literary figures of the day visited Great Tew, and though Lucius Carey left little literary work behind him yet his contemporaries unanimously agree in describing him as "a person of such prodigious parts of learning and knowledge, of that inimitable sweetness and delight in conversation, of so flowing and obliging a humanity" that he must have been a young man of a quality rare in that or any other age.

The Civil Wars put an end to these gatherings of wits and

scholars. As Secretary of State to the ill-fated Charles he was obliged to join in the fighting though his natural tastes were for the arts of peace. He died of a musket shot at the Battle of Newbury and was buried in an unmarked grave for fear his enemies might disturb his last peace. He was thirty-four years old when he died, and that was the end of the Tanfield family in Burford.

The town was just as unfortunate with William Lenthall in the priory as lord of the manor as with Sir Lawrence Tanfield. He was as ruthless in his endeavours for self-advancement and probably learnt from his predecessor how to take advantage of the ignorance of the people when he bought up land they could not afford to enclose. Wood wrote of him: "He minded most the heaping up of riches and was so besotted in raising and settling a family that he minded not the least good that might accrue to his Prince". Allowing for the plain speaking of the times and the malice of the writer there still remains much truth in this statement.

When Lenthall had enlarged the priory he hung it with pictures bought from the dispersed collection of Charles I, including "Queen Henrietta Maria" by Vandyke, "Sir Thomas More and Family" by Holbein. He also built a private chapel. On his deathbed he declared he had never consented to the death of the king but had been misled by Cromwell and his advisers. He must have been haunted by remorse for he ordered that no monument should be built for him but a nameless stone should be placed over his grave.

His ambition for his family came to nothing. He had only one son, Sir John Lenthall, described by Wood as "the grand braggadio and lier of the age he lived in". Other writers of the period make it plain that Sir John was without his father's abilities while inheriting his worst faults. He was first a Parliamentarian, but at the Restoration became a Royalist, and the king with Nell Gwyn, stayed at the priory as his guest.

The priory remained in the Lenthall family until the beginning of the nineteenth century when after being sold and resold, parts of it altered and other parts pulled down, it was left empty and began to fall slowly into ruin. Arthur Gibbs in *A Cotswold Village* describes a visit there. He writes of elder shrubs growing through the broken pavement and the house "but an empty shell, almost as hollow as a skull".

Compton Mackenzie, later, in *Guy and Pauline* builds up a picture of the ruins that would delight the heroine of Northanger Abbey. "The great pile, whose stones the encroaching trees had robbed of warmth and vitality, brooded into the silence with a monstrous ghostliness . . ." With "casements whose glass was filmy like the eyes of dead men or sometimes diced with sinister gaps", and rooms where "the floor had jagged pits and there was not one which was not defiled by jackdaws, owls and bats", he describes a ruin so horrible that one marvels how E. J. Horniman, who bought it in 1912, could have restored it.

This he did, however, even buying Holbein's picture of Sir Thomas More and replacing it on the panelled walls of the ballroom. The Hornimans have gone, but the great house remains. The ghosts of Sir Lawrence Tanfield and Speaker Lenthall would no longer feel at home there so completely have they been forgotten, for they did nothing for the town by which they could be remembered gratefully.

The ford over the Windrush was the reason Burford became a market and halting place in Saxon times for travellers. In the centuries which followed it grew up as a junction of important roads going north, south, east and west. This is best illustrated by its fame in the coaching era when it was a stopping place for the various big coaching concerns serving the length and breadth of the country as the road-books of the time show.

Every town of any antiquity has had one period when it reached its highest peak of prosperity. Burford had never been as necessary to the wool trade as towns like Northleach, Campden and Fairford, and the clothing trade gave it little impetus. It was not until the alarms and excursions of the Civil Wars were over and the initial miseries of the Enclosures abated that Burford found in the coaching trade an industry ennabling it to flourish as it had never done when the lords of the manor were Judge Tanfield and Speaker Lenthall. One of its small industries in the seventeenth century was saddle making, Burford saddles having a reputation far beyond the immediate neighbourhood, and this association with horses and horsemanship had a natural affinity to the town from the beginning.

The coming of the railways ruined the coaching trade and Burford fell on bad times again, its population decreasing and

suffering all the indignities the late nineteenth and early twentieth
centuries could inflict.

Burford has come into its own again now when all the world
goes travelling for pleasure and for profit by motor-coach or car
and once more it is a busy prosperous little town. Not everything
is the same as it used to be. No golden age comes twice to any
place. The "Burford bait", an expression used to describe the
gargantuan meals of the Burford folk can no longer be said to
describe the fare offered to visitors, gentility having crept in.
Also it never occurred to mine hosts of the old days to exploit the
antiquity of their houses, the past being regarded more as an en-
cumbrance than an asset.

X

WILLIAM MORRIS IN THE COTSWOLDS

No portrait of the Cotswolds would be complete without a portrait of William Morris. Though he was unaware of it, and its growth only became apparent after his death, he was in many ways responsible for the Cotswold "cult" of the 1920s. Before his time it was known to few outside the district, but his discovery of the Cotswold vernacular, though it had not yet received this name, and his appreciation of it, had repercussions amongst a wide circle of artists, craftsmen and writers associated with him, who in turn widened the companies of those setting out to explore for themselves this delectable land.

It is the grey stone manor house, Kelmscott Manor, William Morris's country home from 1871 to 1896, which brings the village of Kelmscott into Cotswold country. Here the hills are not the dominant part of the landscape but close the horizons as grey or soft blue distances according to the prevailing skies. The valley trees are here, the elms, poplars, willows and alders, and in the spring the water-meadows are sprinkled with cuckoo-flowers and yellow king-cups. The coot and moorhen are the constant birds, the heron a familiar one, with sedge-warblers to play nightingale. It is country such as the early English water-colourists loved, with wide translucent skies and flat green meadows and no violent contrasts between earth and heaven. It might be truer to say that Kelmscott is the Cotswolds of William Morris set down amongst the lonely reaches of the infant Thames, a place where languorous airs in summer make time stand still and reality merges into dreams.

To the casual eye the village has changed little since William Morris lived there, and Kelmscott House has changed not at all, except that it has lost the owners who loved it well and has become a pre-Raphaelite shrine instead of a home. It is a kind of death but a well-preserved one. When I go to Kelmscott I like to forget the pre-Raphaelites and remember only that this was the home William Morris loved, and the riverside the place where he walked and talked and pondered.

A group of cottages designed by Philip Webb and erected by Jane Morris in memory of her husband keep to the traditional style without being an imitation of it. It is a memorial which would have pleased him for just as the seventeenth-century stone masons often finished their work with a small decorative detail, so one of these cottages has a carving representing William Morris sitting on the ground, his face lifted as if listening to the birds in the branches above him while the background shows the old wool-barn and steep-roofed summer house belonging to the manor house. It expresses a romantic nineteenth-century medievalism quaintly but without sentimentality and like any good ornament on a building reveals the period when the cottages were built. The stone has been kind to it.

As an example of a small Elizabethan house Kelmscott is an architectural jewel, fitting as a home not only for the poet William Morris but for the designer, medievalist, and lover of the English tradition in architecture and rural life. It must have satisfied all these aspects of this many-sided man, who spent his life in pursuit of a practical beauty he wanted everyone to enjoy. I suspect he was often told he was fortunate to have found such a house; I hope one at least of the people who made this remark added that he deserved it. That tiresome question what is beauty was no problem to him; as far as it touched himself and his work he was one of those fortunate people who knew the answer.

He loved every part of it, particularly the roof. "It is covered with the beautiful stone slates of the district, the most lovely covering which a roof can have," he wrote. The slates are still arranged in the pattern originally devised by the builders, that is with small slates on top graduating to the largest ones at the eaves, a pattern best suited to the heavy material and steep pitch of the roof. "It gives me the same sort of pleasure in their orderly beauty as a fish's scales or a bird's feather," he said of it, going to nature as was customary with him for an image to deck his statement.

The house is tall, the walls unrelieved except for the mullioned windows with their moulded drip-stones and gables topped with plain ball finials. The best view of it is from the garden where the

Lower Guiting church

dark yew hedge and bright flower borders make a perfect foil for the old grey stone. There is nothing pretentious, nothing false in its austerity. His own words best describe it: "the type of the pleasant places of the earth, and of the homes of the harmless simple people not overwhelmed by the intricacies of life."

The intricacies of life may not have concerned him but that he delighted in the intricacies of nature is obvious. In the chintzes and hangings he designed one sees a sensitive appreciation of the curl of petal, leaf and tendril and the way they lent themselves to his purpose. It was not so much that he used them but they used him, for time and time again he interprets not only their form and colour but the essence and mood of their being. They are not always typically English flowers, and his designs and colour have nothing in common with peasant art. They are highly civilized, sometimes over-civilized.

His medievalism as expressed in his tapestries, wall-papers and chintzes have nothing to do with the sentimental Merry England Maypole-on-the-Green revival of the early twentieth century, a revival which died of boredom induced by its own mawkishness and which had little to do with the folk. Morris's medievalism had its roots in the East, and again and again one can trace in his colour and patterns the influence of the Persian designs he loved so well.

At times his work seems to contradict the bluff, downrightness of his nature, yet remembering the exotic beauty of the girl he chose for his wife one begins to perceive the pervading nature of his romanticism. The word "romantic" has become debased in the last two decades, but taking it to mean an emphasis towards the strange and foreign, a vivid awareness of the subtleties of the imagination, then there were times when Morris could be thus described.

He was a sturdy man with rugged features and nothing of the aesthete in his appearance. One could not have imagined him "walking down Piccaddily with a poppy or a lily in his medieval hand"; he was more likely to be seen with a tool for like all true craftsmen he delighted in the handling of them.

His creed was that the daily things we use and have about us should be useful as well as beautiful, but he also had the rare quality of tenderness for miniature loveliness. He wanted life to

8

The wolds behind Naunton

be uncomplicated, with everyone healthy, beautifully clad and free to choose their own work. A certain puritanism and love of hard work kept his idealism from being insipid. I think he knew this way of life lacked something for in *News from Nowhere* an insidious melancholy occasionally creeps into the conversation of those bright and beautiful beings he created.

Another link with the Cotswolds as well as the material and style of Kelmscott Manor was that former owners had been engaged in the wool trade and the barn in the manor grounds was originally used for storing wool. A stone fireplace in the great parlour bears the arms of the Turners whose memorials in Kelmscott church go back to 1667. It was from a Miss Turner who married a Hobbs of Maisey Hampton that Morris leased the house in 1871. His wife bought it after his death, and in 1938 when May Morris, their daughter, died, it passed into the care of the University of Oxford. Through the south window Morris could see his domain, "the barn with its beautifully sharp gable, the grey stone sheds and the dovecot . . . the flank of the earlier house and the little gables and grey scaled roofs".

Another building owed its being to William Morris, the village hall erected thirty-seven years after his death as a memorial to him and his work. The stone came from a quarry at Filkins owned by Sir Stafford Cripps, and was a gift. Ernest Gimson drew the plans but did not live to see them materialize, and the actual building was carried out by a local builder, Mr. King of Lechlade, supervised by May Morris, who inherited her father's love of good workmanship and who worked passionately on the project gathering funds to make it possible. When the estimated cost was exceeded she found the money herself so that it should not fall below the standard which would have satisfied her father.

The hall was many years in coming into being, each step being lovingly considered. The site, given by Lord Faringdon, stands back from the road enclosed in a fence of large flat stones set upright and secured with iron bolts, and flanked by dry-stone walling. There is a stone seat beside the door and a protecting stonehead over it; in the gable a mullioned window in the traditional style. Everything is simple, sturdy and well-made.

On the day the hall was opened many famous people, statesmen, writers and artists, came to Kelmscott to pay tribute to William

Morris. To quote one of them: "William Morris's influence is in every stone and every piece of timber in this building". Although the villagers must have been flattered by this appreciation from outside and probably kept a well-mannered silence as they stared at the visitors they probably told each other when the ceremony was over that Mr. Morris belonged to them and not to these important people from London. Had he not elected to be buried in their churchyard under a tombstone that differed very little from those which covered their own people? When I saw it in 1963 its lettering was still as satisfying as ever, a reminder of how much we owe Philip Webb who designed it, and his associates, for a revival of an art which had deteriorated since the eighteenth century.

William Morris loved not only his own corner of the Cotswolds but the whole area. Ever the crusader, he soon began a battle with the church "restorers", for on the Cotswolds as elsewhere many ancient churches were in a poor state after the depressions and wars of the late eighteenth and nineteenth centuries. The restorers had already begun to move in, often imposing an uninspired taste upon the ancient fabrics. Morris was one of the few who had the foresight to see what the country was losing and who took practical steps to prevent it.

Renovations at Burford church roused him to draft a letter of protest in his usual forceful manner. Out of this grew the Society for the Protection of Ancient Buildings, afterwards renamed by him the Anti-Scrape Society. Its motto was "Protection instead of Restoration" and Morris became its secretary. He was technically qualified, having served an early training under Street, and though he forsook architecture as a profession it remained one of his outstanding passions. Time and time again in his books he describes buildings with an imaginative understanding of their architectural points. In a chapter in *A Dream of John Ball* his description of the interior of the church where he talks with the hedge-priest takes a full page and today his picture of the church is more alive than the story.

Mrs. Gretton, in her book on Burford, tells of the fierce controversy which raged between Morris and Mr. Cass, the vicar, over renovations at Burford church. William Morris kept a sense of fun to sweeten his compaigning. Mr. Cass, also a determined man, ended his argument with Morris by saying firmly,

"This church, sir, is mine, and, if I choose to, I shall stand on my head in it," a remark which delighted Morris. G. D. G. Cole once described Morris as one who when he was not making pictures in tapestry, wallpaper, wood or stone, made them in words or in his mind, seeing everything pictorially. This faculty could have translated Mr. Cass's remark into a vision of an upside-down clergyman, a picture having something in common with the medieval grotesques Morris knew so well.

In founding the Society for the Protection of Ancient Buildings Morris did not contemplate it as a small select society dictating to the masses what they should or should not like. "I don't believe in the possibility of keeping art alive by the action, however energetic, of a few groups of specially gifted men and their small circle of admirers amidst a general public incapable of understanding and enjoying their work," he wrote. One wonders what he would think of those artists, poets and musicians of today who alone hold the key to their creative endeavours. I put the question to a modern poet, who replied that it was the work of men like Morris who had brought about the violent reaction against romanticism.

"He was not one who kept his work to himself," I argued.

"Merry England and tumblings in the hay with the realism, the essential truth left out. He knew Ruskin and Rossetti and heaven knows their lives were no innocent idylls. We may go too far in the opposite direction and talk sex instead of love but we do know the poet's lot is not a happy one, as Gilbert might have put it," he replied.

The last time I went to Kelmscott was a hot sunny afternoon in late May, and as I turned into the lane leading to the village it was as if I had been transported back into the years before the war. The village looked empty; there was even a dog stretched full length in the middle of the road fast asleep. No children played, no women gossiped at the cottage doors. There were no shiny cars, no sound of pop singers on the radio. The village was wrapt in a slumbrous haze of heat as in a dream and from the open barn doors came a dry acrid smell of hay and straw and farmyard dust. It might have been sleeping since William Morris first lived there.

I went to the churchyard and found a narrow path through the tall waving grasses had been trodden down, showing others still made the pilgrimage. Bluebells and tulips were in flower in one corner and a clump of columbines, Ophelia's flower, so dark in their sombre purple as to look black in the sunlight. Nature had added a plant of herb robert with bright pink flowers and a tracery of delicate leaves outstretched to make a pattern on the stone.

To have gone into the manor house to see the pious collection of his household treasures as one looks in at a museum would have broken the spell. It was not as a writer, craftsman or social reformer, or as a friend of the pre-Raphaelite painters I wanted to think of him that afternoon but as one who had loved this homely place, for Kelmscott is no show village to attract the casual visitor in search of the picturesque: and that is something for which a village should be thankful today.

I walked along past the manor house aloof behind its wall and closed garden door to the river and sat down on the bank. An occasional large fish jumped to a fly with a plop which sent ripples over the placid shining surface. Martins and swallows swooped to the water in a mingling of curving flights and a spotted flycatcher flew backwards and forwards from his post under a willow, his pale under-parts catching the light each time he made a silent foray out of the shade. Once a small motor boat chugged past, going so slowly that it left only the smallest wake behind.

This sun-drenched afternoon was so unexpected after days of squally wind and rain that it seemed unreal, as if I had slipped back into one of those summers long ago when summer afternoons were always hot and drowsy and there was time to sit on a river bank under the thin-leaved willows and gaze at fields of brilliantly-lit buttercups on the opposite side. I had meant to write my impressions of this corner of Kelmscott, knowing William Morris must have often come here, on foot or by boat, but unless I absorbed them through the skin I was willing to let the trance-like mood keep me idle. After all he himself had described it in *News from Nowhere*, and if I sat an hour or so longer his own words would fit the scene perfectly, "the flat country spreading out far under the sun of a calm evening until something which might have been called hills with a look of sheep pastures about them bounded it by a soft blue line".

The "sheep pastures" bring us back to the Cotswolds.

XI

THE COLN VALLEY

OF the three valleys, the Churn, the Coln and the Leach, whose small rivers come down from their sources in the hills to swell the Thames on its way to Lechlade, the valley of the Coln is the most consistent in its loveliness. The river belongs to the hills and they shelter it most of the way to Fairford. Beyond there, after idling through Fairford Park as a wide water it leaves the hills behind, changing its silvery Cotswold sparkle to meander gently through the flat meadows until it comes to the rushy fields of Inglesham to be lost soon after in the Thames.

It knows every aspect of Cotswold landscape on its way through one small village after another, wearing a different face in every reach within the half dozen or so Cotswold miles it passes before coming to the valley of the young Thames. It can be open in narrow green meadows, secretive between willow-lined banks, unassuming in villages and deep and exciting where it runs under great trees. Whether it is more beautiful when it flows through the heart of the wooded Chedworth region or when it comes to Bibury where the big trout move their tails lazily just below its surface depends on the mood of the day and the onlooker. To its lovers whether they are anglers, naturalists, river-worshippers or just idlers who enjoy a country scene it is always enchanting. Not far from the Chedworth Roman villa the remains of a Roman temple stand on its bank. Was it raised to worship a rural goddess, guardian spirit of the fair life-giving waters?

When the Romans left Britain and the Saxons began to penetrate into the country of the upper Thames they found in the Coln valley a countryside to their liking, with water, timber and a fertile valley soil. Evidence of their earlier settlement exists today in the churches of Coln Rogers and Bibury, and in the Saxon cemetery near Fairford.

One of the pleasantest ways to explore the Coln villages is to leave the Foss Way at Fossbridge and take the minor road winding between stone walls to the secluded village of Coln St. Denis; a road of small delights best enjoyed on foot. For the first quarter mile it keeps high and then begins to dip into the wooded hollow holding the hamlet, the river and the water-meadows. In summer the transition from the drier windier hill country into the moister air and richer soil of the valley is plainly seen. As one descends the vegetation loses its upland lightness, the harebells, scabious and blue meadow cranesbill give place to a darker growth, while the stone walls and roofs are encrusted not only with lichen and moss but are half buried under ivy and box hedges.

The church of St. James with its low heavy tower is dwarfed by great churchyard trees. The ground plan, the doorways and the font are Norman, the north doorway being carved with a billet pattern on the hood mould. On the walls of the nave strange stone heads, carved with crude Norman incisiveness, are corbels which once supported the shafts of the roof. Only a rough field separates the church from the river where dragonflies dart between tall clumps of willow herb and plumes of meadowsweet, and noisy moorhens squawk at one's approach. I always think of Coln St. Denis as the village of wrens, for whenever I have been there I have never failed to see a number of them flitting intently about the ivied walls. There are so many dusty nooks and crannies where a wren can feed and nest.

On the opposite side of the river the tiny hamlet of Calcot, a mere sprinkling of plain stone cottages and farm buildings, clings to the bare hill-slope. It makes a perfect contrast to the richer medieval charms of Coln St. Denis, and sets one marvelling again at the many facets of the Cotswold scene.

Coln Rogers, like Coln St. Denis, is a small tree-shaded village with its ancient church, grey-gabled Elizabethan vicarage and houses set back a little from the water-meadows but with the river as an important part of the picture. Time and the damp valley have darkened the stones of its walls and roofs to a sombre grey which the strongest sunlight fails to brighten. Its church of St. Andrew is one of the oldest in Gloucestershire and as well as keeping the original Saxon plan Saxon work can still be seen in its fabric, pilaster strips, long and short work on the south-east angle of the nave and a Saxon window north of the chancel. The south doorway is Norman with a plain tympanum, and there is a

Norman tub font and chancel arch. Various fragments of old glass include a piece showing a charming little medieval figure of St. Margaret and the dragon. Time has blended all four periods, Saxon, Norman, Early English and Perpendicular into a quiet harmony within the grassy churchyard overhung by trees.

Winson, about a mile from Coln Rogers, is one of the smallest villages in the valley, but it is complete with a small church, a chapelry of Bibury, with a Norman door and chancel arch, a mill, farms and cottages. Willow trees overhanging the water link it to the river, but the massive stone barns are a stronger link with the hills, for they were built to hold the corn or fleeces, or both, produced in the wide upland acres above the shallow valley, and whose long green slopes enclose it. There is something satisfying about a great barn. Its architectural stability is a reassurance of faith in the bounteousness of the earth comforting in an age of small packaging and temporary containers.

From Winson the road winds on to Ablington, the home of Arthur Gibbs. *A Cotswold Village* was published in 1898, before the spate of books relating intimate and personal reactions to Cotswold life and scene began. It is now a classic and deserves to be, for it follows a classical tradition, though the ancient classical writers who retired to their country estates and employed themselves in country pursuits and scholarship did so because they had been banished from the centres of civilization. Life at Ablington was no exile for Arthur Gibbs but one he preferred to all others.

I doubt if *A Cotswold Village* is read today, for the end of the nineteenth century seems more remote from modern life than ancient Greece or Rome. It was the first book on the Cotswolds I read, and though this was many years ago I think of it nostalgically whenever I pass through Ablington. It is also one of those books I dare not read again lest the magic has been lost in the storms of passing years. Any changes one sees in Ablington today, however, are for the better, which is an amazing statement to make when one remembers what has happened to other Cotswold villages.

After crossing the river the temptation is to take the road north to the Salt Way for it is the kind of road which beckons one to follow it into the high wolds especially on a day when the wind is a brisk north-wester and visibility good. But such a day is also one when Bibury can look its best, bringing out the texture of the old grey stone and filling the valley with light reflected from sky and water.

It has become one of the Cotswold show places since William Morris called it the most beautiful village in England and it has not been spoilt by its many visitors. It caters for them without debasing its own charms, and there are occasions in mid-week when one can sit on the low wall of the mile-long main street running with the river without another soul to jostle one's elbow or break the rural peace. The river is no stripling here but has widened out to some thirty feet, spanned by a three-arched stone bridge in whose cool shade big trout linger, looking almost as ancient and speckled as the stone which gives them shelter. This, and the marshy hollow of lush green going back to the shaded backwaters and channels under the wooded hillside and flanked by the old mill and the miniature perfection of Arlington Row's dormers and gables makes it an open village, showing its charms without reserve.

Bibury has another corner not so openly displayed. At the east end on a bank well above the marshy valley stands the church, the manor house, Bibury Court, and a gathering of typical Cotswold cottages. These once stood about a tiny green but this has now been covered with gravel to make a car park for the church.

The original Saxon church was of considerable size and must have been an important meeting place of churchmen in Saxon times. There are still considerable remains of the old church to be seen on the north side of the nave, in the windows and in the jambs of the chancel arch. Outside the north wall of the chancel there is a sculptured stone patterned with interwoven circles and dots thought to be of Scandinavian design. Three other such stones of pre-Norman date were sent to the British Museum in 1913 before it was realized that local treasures were best displayed in their own district.

These tantalizing glimpses of Saxon days make one long to know more about the first church, when it was built and how it appeared when the stone was first quarried and the carving crisp and fresh. Lifted up on its bank well above the river it must have been like a beacon to the surrounding countryside, as shining and silvery grey in the sunlight as the river itself.

Alexander Pope when he was staying at Cirencester Park used

to ride over to Bibury and visit at Bibury Court, whose many-gabled front and embattled bay windows two stories high over-look a gracious park land and the river. Pope, with the restraint of an eighteenth-century poet, described the prospect as pleasing.

Bibury is one of those places which have a tranquillizing effect on visitors as well as anglers. In the past when our visitors from the town showed signs of becoming weary of country life we used to take them there. I cannot be certain whether leaning over a wall watching the fish and the river has a therapeutic effect or whether there is something relaxing in the air but I have known it calm many clever restless minds who believe beauty not consciously arrived at is suspect, and places which attract tourists even more suspect. On one small visitor, however, it had the opposite effect.

On the south side of the river where the road to Cirencester begins to mount the hill there is a mill whose monumental buttresses are so massive that one wonders if its builder feared the mill might collapse into the river unless stoutly upheld. I had been invited to visit a fish farm situated between the mill-stream and the Coln and took a small boy with me who had been left in my care to convalesce after measles. As we gazed into the various ponds containing trout of all sizes the boy, usually a volatile and lively child, became very silent. Feeling his unusually quiet behaviour merited a reward I took him for tea at the Swan, the fisherman's inn at the far end of the main street, resolved not to behave like one who knew how many cakes were good for a small boy. He did not seem to appreciate this indulgence though he took advantage of it. I soon became aware he was nursing a secret anger and I was the cause.

After tea I suggested we bought some small toy in the village shop to take home as a souvenir, but he refused to be placated.

"What's the matter?" I asked, unable to bear his displeasure any longer.

Giving me the look of one who had lost all faith in the adult mind he replied bitterly:

"You might have told me we were going to see all those little fishes and I could have taken my bucket and net!"

Then determined to punish me in the only way he knew he added: "And I'm not going to take my tonic tonight, so there!"

Fairford, situated on a river crossing not far from the highest point where the river is navigable and at the end of the Welsh Way's descent from the hills, was one of the earliest Saxon settlements in the Upper Thames valley. Over a hundred years ago in a field close to the town a Saxon cemetery was uncovered and 150 skeletons and a large collection of grave goods were found. It was from these things the authorities deduced that the Saxons were living in Fairford in the sixth century. According to Wylie who conducted the excavations some of the men were 6 feet 6 inches tall, a few even taller. In many of the graves an iron knife was found, in others bronze and gilt brooches. There was no sign that the bodies had been coffined but all the skeletons were perfect.

Bronze bowls, pottery, spearheads, coloured beads, shield bosses, knives, shears and two handsome swords were among the finds. One can imagine the excitement of the local people when the cemetery was uncovered. It was a giants' graveyard, one old road-man told me many years ago, a garrulous old man who would stand and search his memory for tales he had been told about the old days, for he dearly loved an audience. I could tell by the way he spoke that he was still stirred by the thoughts of those giant bones and that they had become entangled in his mind with childhood stories of Jack the Giant-killer, perhaps, or those wicked ogres who cried "Fee, Fi, Fo, Fum" when they smelt the blood of an Englishman.

His father had helped in the excavation, he told me, but strangely enough when I asked him where the field lay he could not remember; he had transplanted it to fairyland. All I could discover after persistent questioning and listening as patiently as I could to his long rambling statements was that long ago cottages had been built on it.

In Domesday the manor of Fairford is called "Terra Regis" but after belonging to the crown it belonged to various families, to the Clares, Earls of Gloucester, the younger Hugh Despencer, the Beauchamps, and finally, in the late fifteenth century, a wealthy wool merchant, John Tame, bought it from Henry VII, to whom it had reverted.

John Tame and his family dominated the town for many years. According to Leland this "praty uplandisch town never flourished afore the Cumming of the Tames onto it". John Tame, with the example of other Cotswold wool-men at Northleach and Campden in mind, set about rebuilding the church in the accepted Perpendicular style, filling its windows with the painted glass which has made Fairford church famous. The guardians of the church have always taken steps to keep it safe in times of war and it has miraculously survived the hazards of the years from its first removal during the Civil Wars when the rector had it taken away and hidden until it was safe to put it back again. It is hard to understand why the Puritans should have wanted to destroy it, for the western windows forming a great triptych of Judgement with its gloomy, sadistic rendering of the torments of hell far overweighs the delights of heaven, as if terror rather than love of God inspired it.

Having once spent over three hours with neck craned upward listening to an expert lovingly describe the windows inch by inch I suggest the interested reader obtains the excellent booklet on sale in the church and studies this wonderful painted glass in several sessions with intervals for rest and refreshment. Otherwise one finds oneself concentrating on the hideous activities of the devils and missing the charming glimpses of pastoral scenes forming the background of some of the pictures. Many of these, it is said, were derived from the landscape about the town and river.

There are some good brasses in the church, for John Tame (died 1500) in traditional wool-men fashion had his effigy and that of his wife thus represented on his tomb. Another brass of his son Sir Edmund Tame (died 1534) his two wives and family lies on the floor near the altar steps.

The choir stalls have some amusing misericords; the woodcarvers do not seem to have been so overawed by the pictures in the windows that they could not indulge in a little bucolic humour. One shows a tipsy couple drinking from a barrel, the man urging the woman with his foot. In another a woman holds a boy by the hair and is beating him with a flat stick, her attitude expressing that overspill of exasperation which has been the theme of the comic throughout the ages.

Sir Edmund Tame, John Tame's son, was also a church builder. St. Peter's at Rendcomb was rebuilt by him, and his initials are to be seen on the corbels and on some old glass in a window in the nave. Fortunately he left the circular Norman font with its fret band ornament and arcades containing the twelve apostles, eleven recognizable and the twelfth a shapeless figure probably intended for Judas, one of the most interesting fonts on the Cotswolds.

Fairford is a pleasant old-fashioned country town more concerned with its own affairs and the fishermen than with casual tourists. American airmen stationed not far away and men from other Cotswold air-fields in the district brought an unusual animation to its quiet streets for a few years during the last war, but now it looks as if it could easily slip into obscurity as it did in the days between the passing of the wool trade and the coming of the coaching era.

Fortunately the church on its knoll with only a road between the churchyard and the green depths of Fairford Park, the square containing the old coaching inns and a row of stone houses of every period from the early eighteenth century to late Victorian lie off the main road and one can walk there in comfort. It is a pity the bridge over the river cannot play a more distinguished part in the town's make-up. A view of the water and its meadows would give grace to the little town, but the busy main road passing over it makes this impossible and coming into Fairford one is generally over the bridge before one realizes the river lies below. To most of the traffic passing through the town Fairford must look like a small village.

The church tower has some interesting trade symbols and reminders of the great families who once owned the manor. John Tame was determined all should be remembered. On the south side are the arms of Warwick with the Warwick ragged staff and the Yorkist shut fetlock, on the east a muzzled bear climbing the ragged staff and above a shield with the three chevrons of the de Clares who held the manor in the thirteenth century. John Tame's merchant's mark is on the north side, also two horse-shoes and pincers, gryffons, a wine vat, scissors, a hunter's horn and baldrick. On the west side, above the strange archaic-looking figure of Christ of Pity is a shell, the emblem of the salt trader, taking us back to the days when salt was carried from Droitwich across the Cotswolds and then along the Welsh Way to the river where it was then shipped to London. Shears and gloves and the armorial bearings of John Tame himself, a wyvern combating a lion complete the series. There does not seem very much about the town, its owners and occupations that John Tame left out when the tower was built.

The figure called Christ of Pity is the most arresting of them all, with his right hand uplifted in blessing and holding in his left hand the Resurrection Cross. It helps to nullify a little the ferocity of the demons and devils tormenting sinners in the painted glass windows.

Kempsford, three miles south of Fairford, is not on the Coln but the Thames, and with a little tolerance could be claimed as coming into the outermost fringe of Cotswold. It has at least one lovely old Cotswold house, some picturesque cottages, a grouping of farm buildings as handsome and massive as any to be found in the heart of the region and in the church a fine brass to Walter Hickman, wool-stapler, his wife who bore the charming name of Corystan, and their four sons.

Before the concentration of hutments and other utilitarian buildings enclosed by a forbidding wire fence round Whelford had cast its gloom over the winding lanes between Fairford and Kempsford I could never resist leaving the main road to visit the village on my way to Cirencester from the south. The quiet lanes always held some little surprise, a snipe zigzagging over the flat lonely meadows, a heron rising behind a hedge, a skein of ducks across the sky, or some other sign that one was not far away from the waterside.

Kempsford has more associations with kings and nobles than with the wool trade direct, though I dare say much of their wealth came from the wool trade. The history of the village goes back into the Dark Ages, tradition saying that a Saxon palace or stronghold belonging to the Mercians stood here facing land on the other side of the river in the days when England was divided into small kingdoms. It may well have been so for this was border territory for the two kingdoms, and the fords along the river strategic points in their fluctuating frontiers.

Some five or six centuries later a castle stood here belonging to Maud, the wife of Henry Plantagenet, third earl of Lancaster and grandson of Henry III. Edward I was entertained at the castle and Edward II during his quarrel with the barons was brought here as prisoner and placed in the Earl of Lancaster's charge. An old story tells that Maud died by her husband's hand because he wrongly believed her false to him and that her ghost haunted the castle. Another variant, and there are many, is that her ghost walks on the terrace of the ancient mansion, now disappeared, but as the mansion was built at least a century later it seems, as so often happens in old tales, that names and events have become telescoped into one romantic episode. It is such a tale as village folk remembered when the mists covered Lady Maud's Walk, between the vicarage garden and the river, with swirling wraiths of ghostly white. But that was in the days before cinema and television screens provided far more horrifying stories to chill the blood.

Another noble lady comes into the Kempsford stories. This was Blanche, the first wife of John of Gaunt, who built the handsome tower of the church in her memory. Lady Blanche was patroness of Chaucer, and one of his earlier poems, "The Deth of Blaunche, the Duchesse," was written after she died of the Plague in 1369.

In the poem Chaucer makes the mourning duke tell how he first met his wife, and though we do not know if John of Gaunt ever described this to Chaucer it is easy to imagine that the poet was using the death of his noble patroness as a means of expressing his love for another woman. The verses have such undeniable evidence of warmth, freshness and true emotion that one knows they come from his heart and were not made for the occasion as part of his duties. Even allowing for a poet's skill in embroidering such a theme as the early death of a beautiful woman, Lady Blanche emerges as a true and lovely woman, and the simplicity of:

> joye get I never none
> Now that I see my ladye bright
> Which I have loved with all my might,
> Is from me dead and is agone,

suggests that his sorrow at her death was more than a poet's fancy or regret for the loss of a patroness.

Time has not been kind to Kempsford, and only at the far end of the village where the church stands half hidden from view by the tall trees of the burial ground and churchyard does it still dream of the past. The long straggling village street deteriorates once it has passed the insignificant bridge over the choked and weedy canal and is in a state of transition between the modern world and the old; so far neither has emerged with certainty.

XII

THREE TOWNS ON THE FOSS WAY

NORTHLEACH, Stow on the Wold and Moreton in Marsh all owe their existence, or their continued existence, to their position on or near the Foss Way. Stow, a hill-top town, is the oldest of the three and was on the line of a Cotswold ridgeway in existence long before the Romans came, while the Foss Way actually passes through Moreton as its main street and it is believed that there was some kind of settlement there in prehistoric times.

The first mention of Northleach is in 1227, when the Abbot of Gloucester obtained a market grant and detached 500 acres from his manor of Eastington to set up the town. Situated just off the Foss Way in a deep steep-sided coombe at the head of a valley, there was room in the valley bottom only for one long narrow street. The Market Square is on the site of the quarry out of which stone for the original town was taken, thus eating into the steep slope and providing a little more flat space where the town could expand, while above the Market Square where the ground rises again room on a hillside terrace was found for the church, a farm and a few larger houses.

The old Market House, still in existence in 1804, stood near the present post office, with the market cross near by, but both have gone and been forgotten. The Blind House where prisoners were housed still remains, a fact which might typify in grim fashion the later melancholy history of Northleach when its wool trade had vanished and it fell on bad times. Around the town are miles of rolling uplands, once famous sheep walks but now mostly under the plough. It was wool and sheep which gave Northleach its medieval prosperity and its famous church.

It is difficult to say anything new about the church of St. Peter and St. Paul. Not only does it belong to the town but it was made out of it. Built in the middle of the fifteenth century in the Perpendicular style it has a clerestoried nave of five bays, north and

128

A house at Burford

south aisles and chapels, a chancel with a north chapel, a high embattled western tower and a south porch both massive and graceful, everything, in fact, that the wool-men could give it. Their memorial brasses with their effigies and merchants' marks lie in the nave. There is also a brass of an earlier unknown wool-man and his wife thought to have come from the earlier church. John Fortey, Thomas Bushe, John Taylour, Will Midwinter are all there in the church they helped to build.

The porch of two bays with the glorious vaulted roof is arcaded on the lateral walls, while the south front has two central canopied stone niches holding figures of the Holy Trinity and a Virgin and Child. Fortunately these escaped Sir Thomas Fairfax's soldiers quartered in the town after the Battle of Naseby. There is an upper chamber lit by four windows and reached by an octagonal staircase, its fireplace and chimney adapted cleverly from a butt-ress with an open crocheted pinnacle.

In recent years it has been necessary to repair a leaking roof, replace timbers eaten by deathwatch beetles and make other expensive repairs. The townspeople are unable to bear the heavy cost themselves, but fortunately the fame of Northleach church reaches beyond the town and beyond the Cotswolds and the appeal for help comes to all who would save an ancient church.

It would seem that only the wool-men cherished the town. When they were dead and their trade with them it dwindled almost into oblivion. By the end of the fifteenth century its name ceased to be known in the markets of the Continent, though the name of Midwinter, connections of the wool factor we learn so much about in the Cely Papers, has persisted in the town for cen-turies. A plentiful water supply was necessary for the clothing trade which developed in the following centuries and unlike the Stroudwater district Northleach had only the muddy trickle of the infant Leach. In 1608, according to *The Return of Men and Armour for Gloucestershire* Northleach had five weavers while in Cirencester and other places in the south Cotswolds hundreds of weavers found employment.

Fascinating evidence of the town's life from 1547 to 1688 can be found in the Court-Book of Northleach which managed to sur-vive those years when municipal authorities and others were not aware of the valuable material for the historian existing in the

9

Northleach church from the south

dusty records of the past. The Court was a combination of Court Leet and Municipal council, consisting of a bailiff, town-clerk, sergeant-at-arms, two constables and other officers of minor degree, and every tradesman in the town was obliged to attend.

As well as public affairs the private conduct of the townsfolk came under review and the Court had power to punish offenders by chastisement, pillory, stocks, imprisonment and fines. There are such entries as the payment of sixpence for faggots to burn the "measley piggs", which tells its own tale, and fines to bakers for "wanting in the peny lofe". Apprentices who stayed out after nine o'clock in winter and ten in summer could be punished by spending all night in the stocks. It also required those attending the Court to appear "in gowns and other decent upper garments", and going to church on Sunday without a cap brought a fine of twopence. A weaver is fined sixpence for playing "coytes" during Divine Service. Anyone found using any other but the "fore-street" door of the inn was liable to a fine of five shillings and as the inns were opened from early morning until late at night this rule makes one wonder if sneaking in by the back door had a more sinister intent than thirst.

It is from the Court-Book one learns that Charles I was at Northleach in 1643, for a Widow Westmancott received a rent rebate of twenty-four shillings for supplying oats to the constables for the king's use. In 1645 after the Battle of Naseby Sir Thomas Fairfax and his army were quartered in the town. The soldiers broke open the Town Box, no doubt expecting to find money, and then in wanton mischief destroyed pages of the Court-Book and indulged in other forms of destruction. The townspeople must have watched them march away with great relief. Not being a prosperous town the depredations of the soldiers brought real hardship.

We know there was much poverty and unemployment. William Dutton, the brother of Thomas Dutton, who founded and endowed the six little almshouses early in the century, left the Great House and £200 to be used by "some honest tradesman in freestains or stuffs or in any other such trade as may keep the people from idleness".

Being on the high road to Oxford and Cheltenham as well as just off the Foss Way Northleach revived as a posting town during the rise of the coaching trade, but with the coming of the railways it declined again, no railway coming within seven miles of it. The great expansion in motor transport in the last twenty years has not been altogether beneficial, though it has put the town on the map again. The cars, vans, lorries, buses roar along the main street in a never-ceasing procession, with a preponderance of heavy commercial vehicles.

If one comes into the town from east or west along the congested highway the first glimpses are not impressive, though there is an exciting view of the magnificent church tower to be seen just before turning off the Foss Way. Northleach, however, improves on acquaintance, particularly if one comes to it on foot from Farmington in the north or from Helen's Ditch in the south, or by taking a gentle rising path along one side of the Market Square out of the roar of the traffic to the ridge where the church stands, gracious and commanding above the town.

Here there is room to walk and look at the same time, and a splendid old barn with long window slits and four staggered rows of pigeon holes between two string courses running the whole length of the side overlooking the churchyard shows that one has come into the Cotswold world again. On this ridge there are also a few pleasant stone houses, but when one remembers that Northleach was once the most important wool-mart in the central Cotswolds it is disappointing to find so few domestic dwellings of any distinction. The size and beauty of the church leads one to expect so much more. Where did they live, these wealthy woolmen who built it, John Fortey, Will Midwinter the factor, John Taylour, Thomas Bushe and the others whose memorial brasses are amongst the smaller treasures in the church? Some houses may have been pulled down during bad times when it was cheaper to destroy than repair, while others have been disguised by commonplace façades and alterations.

When I went to Northleach years ago the prison at the crossroads where the Foss meets the Cheltenham-Burford road always cast a gloom over me before I actually reached the town. After reading a chapter on Sir George Onesipherous Paul by Dr. E. A. L. Moir in *Gloucestershire Studies* I can now look at it with better understanding though I cannot pretend that its squat square shape gives me any pleasure. Logically, I suppose, as its original purpose was not to enhance the landscape but keep secure the unfortunates incarcerated within its walls one should not expect a prison to look like a palace or any kind of pleasant dwelling. Taking it a step further the prisoners themselves could object to being confined in a place whose outside appearance suggested dignity or grace when within it was ugly and depressing. Whatever the answer, the building makes an unhappy beginning to the town, though today it is no longer used as a prison and now has a bright trim frontage.

When it was built, however, by the efforts of Sir George Onesipherous Paul, it was an improvement on the Houses of Correction common in the county. When one reads of the appalling conditions in those places with prisoners so closely confined that typhus and other gaol-fevers killed off more occupants than served their sentences, of men and women herded together like animals without privacy of any kind and the hardened criminals placed with those committed for small offences, one finds it difficult to understand why such degrading cruelty did not arouse greater outcry. To quote Howard, the famous prison reformer, on only two of Gloucestershire prisons, "At St. Briavel's Castle . . . no yard: no water: no allowance: no firing: One sickly creature confined a twelvemonth and never once put out of that dismal room." And of the prison at Winchcombe where the keeper confessed because of the state of the building "he should be obliged to put irons on all the prisoners to secure them".

Sir George Onesipherous Paul came of a family of south Cotswold clothiers originally of Huguenot descent. His father had a flourishing business at Woodchester and became one of the leading citizens of the district. As High Sheriff of Gloucester he presented a loyal address on the accession of George III and so received a knighthood. Twelve years later he was created a baronet, thus following the pattern of advancement of other wealthy Cotswold clothiers.

Onesipherous was born at Woodchester and received the education of a young gentleman of the period, finishing with Oxford and the Grand Tour. The account books he kept, probably at his father's request, recently deposited in the Gloucestershire Records Office show that he behaved like any other young man of taste and leisure. Ruffles, canes, snuff-boxes, an embroidered silk coat and velvet waistcoat were among his purchases and the loss of considerable sums by betting are recorded with apparent nonchalance. During the Tour he collected pictures and engravings as a gentleman should to take home and adorn his rooms. When his formal education was finished he settled down at home keeping a stable of a dozen horses and supporting the local races, with a town house where he occupied himself with the affairs of the Dilettante Society when country life became tedious. He was extravagant and generally managed to exceed the generous allowance from his father by several hundred pounds a year. He showed no sign whatever of developing a social conscience. If his father hoped he would marry into an aristocratic family and so continue the family's ascent up the social ladder he must have been disappointed; his son remained a bachelor.

When his father died he moved to Hill House at Rodborough, handed over the management of the family mills to his cousin Obadiah and became a country gentleman interested in agriculture and county affairs generally. Unlike the usual run of country gentlemen he also employed his time with his library and picture gallery. In 1780 he became High Sheriff for Gloucestershire and this marked a sobering change in his character and pursuits. To quote Dr. Moir: "The gay, irresponsible, extravagant Onesipherous Paul disappears, and in his place we find that impressive figure Sir George Onesipherous Paul, known to his contemporaries for his good works, his lengthy oratory, and his devotion to the cause of prison reform."

There is no doubt that when he began to study criminal law and the state of the prisons he was deeply shocked. "By REFORM I mean nothing less than a general and entire Correction of the Principle of the Prisons, as well as those for the Lesser as for the Greater crimes," he wrote in 1783. From that time he worked unceasingly, organizing, planning, preparing resolutions for his fellow-justices, delivering long and fervent orations at every public assembly, writing pamphlets and publishing reports. In all his work he was influenced by John Howard. A catalogue of his library shows that he kept himself informed of all the latest developments abroad as well as at home.

It was Howard who introduced him to William Blackburn, a prison architect, and together they planned a new county prison at Gloucester and four smaller ones which included the prison at Northleach. This consisted of a keeper's house, a turnkey's lodge with bath and fumigating rooms, infirmary, chapel, separate courtyards for exercise, day-rooms and cells. "Bread, water, and air, as the means of healthful existence, should be denied to no prisoner," he declared, and that he found it necessary to fight for such elementary necessities throws a dreadful light on the state of the prisons of the times. His *Rules, Orders and Regulations for the Control and Government of Prisons*, which went into four editions, is written in massive prose, the rounded sentences sonorous as his name and loaded with italics and parenthesis. Despite his pompous and egotistical manner and the tedium of his long discourses his sincerity and determination won through and he finally became recognized as a leading authority on prison reform throughout the country.

He is more elegantly remembered by a white marble sarcophagus finished with his bust in Gloucester Cathedral, and an inscription which concludes "For to the object of this memorial is to be ascribed that this county has become an example and model of the best system of criminal discipline in which provident regulation has banished the use of fetters and health has been substituted for contagion, thus happily reconciling humanity with punishment, and the prevention of crime with individual reform".

If Northleach had no clothing trade to give work to its inhabitants it had a prison built under the auspices of the famous eighteenth-century prison reformers.

Towards the end of the nineteenth century it had become a "very Radical town" according to Arthur Gibbs. When one realizes it had known no resident lord of the manor since the Duttons in the early seventeenth century when the town was already in decay this is understandable. Fending for themselves through bad times and good engendered a sturdy and independent spirit and a tough individuality as apparent today as when Arthur Gibbs, facing two hundred "red-hot Radicals" when he was chairman at a Unionist meeting and unable to make them listen to the speakers sang to them instead and was rewarded by enthusiastic cheers. If they did not care for his politics they approved of the way he handled the situation.

The nine miles of the Foss Way from Northleach to Stow on

the Wold is one of the finest stretches of modernized Roman road on the Cotswolds, its only two deviations being where the cross-roads meet the old Puesdown coach road, used by the "Flying Coaches" to avoid the Leach valley, about a mile from the town and again two miles on where it dips to Broadwater Bottom and then comes back into its line to run direct to Stow. It is a high road undulating between 500 and 600 feet all the way. As it comes to the steep rise leading to the town it has tall trees on high banks on each side so that one comes into Stow through a great green tunnel. This makes an excellent contrast to the openness of the town on its hill-top particularly when its streets are filled with the brilliant penetrating light which is one of Cotswold's special attractions.

Stow on the Wold lies close against the Foss for all to see. It has always been a place of call for travellers but in recent years it has been changing into a tourist centre after the manner of Broad-way, though its injudicious use of brightly coloured paint to attract the sightseer into its new cafés and hotels which destroys the subtle tones of the old grey stone would not be tolerated by the more discreet hoteliers and shopkeepers of Broadway. But then they are out to catch a different kind of customer than those who once used the comfortable old-fashioned inns of Stow where on market and fair days farmers and other local people filled them to overflowing and the talk was of horses, cattle, sheep and pigs, the price of barley, local politics and the latest iniquities of the Ministry of Agriculture. Stow has entered into the business of attracting the passing motorist, the visitors with time to kill and money to spend, the modern kind of traveller, in fact, who journeys for amusement. Out of season Stow reverts to its old quiet ways.

From north, south, east and west the roads come in to meet near the town centre. Long before the turnpikes or the Roman Foss Way were made the great Cotswold ridgeway passed near it, and Stow on the Wold where the winds blow cold, though it had not then acquired its present name, must have been often remembered for the penetrating winds which sweep across its great hill.

The Saxons called it by an unpronounceable name from which Maugersbury is derived, and it was given by them with 3,000 acres to Evesham Abbey. In 1107 Henry I decreed that

"Edwardstow" should have a weekly market, and two centuries later the Abbot of Evesham was granted the right to hold a fair in the town. From its earliest beginnings Stow has been a market town supplying the surrounding villages and farms as well as providing food and lodging for travellers.

It grew up naturally about the wide market place, being more fortunate than Northleach in having this flat space on its hill-top. The picturesque alley-ways leading off it came later as more accommodation was needed. The market place enclosed on four sides by shops and houses with a great elm tree for shade, a small town hall in its centre, is still the heart of the town and busy every day as a parking place for the cars and coaches of sightseers from all parts of the country. Making a note at random of the many different place-names on the coaches I put down Lancashire, Wilts and Dorset, Scotland, Bedford and Northants, during one brief afternoon visit.

One of the most handsome houses in the square is St. Edward's House, its tall flat front ornamented by fluted pilasters with a niched doorway reached by shallow steps. At the base of these steps the pilasters used to end in a pair of stone boots, but in recent years the boots have disappeared and a plain moulding put in their place. They were probably an intrusion on the original building but I feel sorry they have gone because there are so few touches of humour in stone on secular buildings and some Cotswold mason must have put them there to amuse himself or his customer.

The tower of St. Edward's church is visible above the trees for miles around but it does not dominate the town itself and one could easily pass through without noticing it. The original foundation was about 870, when it was dedicated to St. Edward the martyr, predecessor of Ethelred, but it has been much rebuilt since then, the first of its great reconstructions being in the fourteenth century when it was rededicated to Edward the Confessor, and a century later when the wealthy wool-merchants raised the great tower and lightened the interior with a clerestory and new windows.

Captain Hasting Keyte, one of the Keytes of Ebrington near Campden, killed at the Battle of Stow in 1646, lies in the chancel; it is possible that some of the Royalist prisoners including old Sir Jacob Astley and hundreds of his men confined in the church after they had surrendered to the Cromwellians envied his fate. An hour spent with the Collection of Civil War Relics in the Town Hall Museum can give a vivid picture of this unhappy period when the shopkeepers and other inhabitants of Stow must have often deplored the fact their town was on a high road and thereby open to the marauding visits of soldiers of both parties.

The four miles of the Foss Way between Stow and Moreton in Marsh run downhill all the way, an area of dry gravel making a firm crossing for the road over the infant Evenlode, a river whose valley and villages inspired Hilaire Belloc and Edward Thomas to write charming lyrics about them but whose beauty is not apparent in the vicinity of the town.

Between the two wars when the Cotswolds were being discovered Moreton in Marsh came low on the list of places to be visited by those in search of typical Cotswold charm. The Foss was one of the routes by which one entered the Cotswolds from Oxford and passing through Moreton one saw it as a sleepy, rather drab little place, pleasant because its wide main street gave it a spacious air but with no special grouping of picturesque old cottages, no gracious manor house or church raised by wealthy wool-men to please the eye. Its name, also, was no recommendation in the pursuit of the picturesque or the hills. An earlier one, Moreton Hindmarsh, meaning marc or boundary, best describes it, though being situated in the damp lowlands it is easily understood how it finally resolved itself into Moreton in Marsh.

The fact that Charles I slept in the White Hart Inn is accepted but not plugged as an attraction for tourists. It has never made any pretence of reverencing the past or of cashing in on it and that is its attitude today. One might ask what has the past done for Moreton and receive a dusty answer.

Until John Freeman, Baron Resedale, purchased the manorial right about 1830 it had belonged to Westminster Abbey, a gift from Edward the Confessor, and never had a landlord who cherished it. Lord Resedale restored the old Market House on its rounded pillars, a building which breaks up the straightness of the Foss and provides a focal point, otherwise one could look right through the town.

It fell on evil times when its wool and weaving trade disappeared and by the end of the eighteenth century its population had dwindled to less than 600, though in the middle of the century a Mr. Busby introduced a linen-cloth business, flax being grown locally at that time. This, however, did little to improve the town and Mr. Busby is remembered only because he decorated his house and garden in the High Street with carved stones and figures from the old ruined Moreton church. But as this kind of decoration is still being applied to many other houses on Cotswold restored to look antique it seems a little hypercritical to condemn him for it. Mr. Busby, however, was more fortunate in that the cost of old carved stones and figures has risen sharply since his day.

To the villages in the neighbourhood it was à market town where groceries and household goods could be bought a little cheaper than elsewhere, a place where at the shop selling antiques one could also pick up cheap second-hand furniture and junk of all kinds including books spotted with damp from the twopenny box and bargains in china and old iron. It was saving the shillings and pence that mattered most in Moreton in the old days; when there was a depression in the farming world Moreton reflected it.

During the last war the R.A.F. stationed in the district brought new life to the town and since then, sharing in the general prosperity of the countryside it has become a busy, prosperous place, catering for travellers because of its position on a main road but not self-consciously occupied in attracting them.

When the Foss Way leaves Moreton it soon leaves Gloucestershire and comes into Oxfordshire. It also leaves behind the more typical Cotswold country though it rises again to the stone country of the Oxfordshire hills when it has left the broad valley of the Evenlode.

XIII

VILLAGES OFF THE FOSS WAY

THE minor roads leading off the Foss Way, well-surfaced and pleasant for driving along if one is satisfied with a moderate speed, are also inviting for those who would explore the lesser-known villages on foot. One rarely encounters more than local traffic except at week-ends. They are never straight enough to become monotonous but rise and dip, make abrupt turns or gentle curves without apparent reason, all the time promising another prospect round the corner and drawing one on.

Walking along them there is time to take in the foreground and background and see a village complete in its setting. Sometimes one is rewarded by finding a stile and footpath making a short cut across fields, though these grow fewer each year, and this gives one a more intimate first view, for the path seldom comes out into the village street but slips into a narrow alley round the backs of cottages leading to the pub, if the village possesses one. Then there is a rest, a drink and sometimes conversation to add to the pleasure of one's walk.

It is in the hill villages that one notices again and again how the old cottages were placed to take advantage of every small fold and hollow that would fit them smugly into the hillside. The churches stand out more boldly, most of them being set on a knoll or ridge, their grey towers showing above the dark mass of churchyard trees, and it is the trees, planted to break the force of the winds blowing unceasingly across the wide fields that make each village an oasis in the bare rolling uplands. The beech with its grey smooth trunks gleaming with a pewter-like lustre are best suited to the wolds. Conifers, whose tops grow ragged and gaunt give a dramatic finish to the skyline but suggest a hungry desolate land-scape and though the hills can be bleak in bad weather their subtle contours have their own grace. In summer, or at any time of the year, with the wind rippling the great wheat and barley fields the scene is one of bounteousness flowing on mile after mile into the horizon.

Each village has its own residue of the past as well as the individuality of its setting to please the eye. Hampnett, a mile northwest of Northleach, small as it is divides itself into two parts, the church, a group of massive farm buildings including a barn and a splendid cart-lodge at the east end, and over the hill homely gatherings of cottages about a sloping green. The church has a Norman chancel and a north doorway with a diapered tympanum. A pair of pelican-like birds with their heads coming together over a small bowl are carved on the capitals on each side of the west archway leading into the chancel reminding one again how the responsiveness of the stone tempted the masons to add touches of fantasy and the grotesque to their work.

Hampnett once stood on the main coaching route between Oxford and Gloucester until the route was diverted through Northleach at the coming of the turnpikes. The passing of the great swaying coaches must have been waited for and watched by the children of the village and their names noted in the same way as they watch the aeroplanes from Cotswold's many airfields roaring through the sky today.

Northward from the last cottage on the edge of the green the road comes to Turkdean in about a mile, dipping down to the leafy lower end of the village sheltered in a fold which also holds a stream to make Lower Dean a place where moss grows soft and thick on stone and tree-trunk and vegetation flourishes. Then the road curves upward and approaches Turkdean through a magnificent avenue of beeches. The church stands off to the right down a short walk, its Norman tower half hidden by tall trees. At the end of the one village street where the road begins to fall again a neat semi-circle of council houses of pale grey artificial stone make a contrast to the dark stone of older cottages. But the gardens of old and new are bright with flowers in their season and bring both old and new together.

Notgrove lies two miles to the north, the road bordered by windbreaks of conifers and beeches alternatively as it climbs slowly to nearly 800 feet. In the centre of the village by the beautifully restored manor house and tiny church with its octagonal spire one is not conscious of being so high on the wolds for elms, hawthorns, lime trees and the clipped yews flanking the entrance to the manor house and church enfold it in greenery.

The church, drastically restored, shows traces of its early origin. On the exterior wall of the east end is a roughly carved Crucifixion about twenty inches high under a worn decorated canopy of a later period, probably thirteenth or fourteenth century. Inside it has an arcade of three Norman arches between nave and aisle, and a simple round font with cable moulding under the rim.

One of the effigies brought in from the churchyard where it had lain for many years was once believed to be that of the last Abbot of Gloucester who retired to Notgrove after the Dissolution. The figure with its cowled habit cut in a series of deep V shapes spreading larger until they reach the feet resting on a small dog would appear to be of the fourteenth century and therefore of too early a date. The simplicity of the lines and the melancholy grey of the weatherworn stone make it look even more remote in time.

Members of the Whittington family, who are supposed to be descended from the Dick Whittington who heard the bells telling him he would be thrice Lord Mayor of London, have effigies of Elizabethan and Stuart date in the chancel. The smallness of the church, the richness of its furnishings, its position practically in the gardens of the manor house make it belong more to the big house than to the village.

To reach Cold Aston and get on to the Foss again the road makes a sharp right-angled turn after leaving the few last cottages scattered on the open wolds. It is here one becomes aware of Notgrave's situation high on the bare uplands. This outer fringe of the village seems to have little connection with the snugly enclosed area about the manor house, and this was brought home to me vividly one early autumn evening many years ago.

I was walking from Northleach to Cold Aston where some friends were meeting me, and as so often happens on Cotswold I had been beguiled by this and that on the way and lost all sense of the passing of time. Dark clouds in the west shutting off most of the light from the afterglow and a cold chilly wind made me aware not only of my careless disregard of time but of the loneliness of the landscape.

As I passed the last cottage a troop of ragged children and an ill-tempered dog rushed out of a garden, the dog snarling and barking, the children waving sticks and shouting rude threatening words. If it had been the middle of the day they would have looked less menacing but in the fading light their uncouth appearance and voices were intimidating, suggesting not a childish game but a deliberate onslaught. A sluttish woman in the cottage doorway with elf locks blowing in the wind and great bare arms folded on her chest was almost more frightening for she looked on indifferently, making no attempt to curb their wild play.

Yelling and whooping they came on like a herd of stampeding young cattle; their faces caught in the yellow beams coming from under the low cloud were wide-mouthed and contorted. I was too weary to run even if it had been wise to do so. I stopped and faced them, making ready to swing my satchel in the face of the dog whose horrid fangs and stiff bristle of hair along his bony spine terrified me far more than the children. It was obvious that this chasing of a stranger was no game to him and he meant to have his bite first.

A stone struck the ground at my feet and this sparked off my anger. I began to advance, shouting to the woman to call the dog off and restrain the children. I was amazed my voice should sound so shrill when my throat was tight with fear. My shout was answered by an angry bellow as a man came out of the cottage, pushing the woman roughly aside as he did so. He swore loudly at the children and they hesitated. The dog, however, still advanced until another shout and a well-aimed clod of earth sent it crawling on its stomach into the long grass at the edge of the road. The man shouted and waved at me to go on, and with a curious pricking of the spine I did so, though it was an effort to turn my back and continue on my way without running. For a few seconds I expected another stone or the dog slinking up behind me for a nip at my ankles but nothing happened.

A violent quarrel between the man and woman had begun. I could hear her loud shrewish voice and his deeper one, but no sound from the children who had evidently found the argument between their elders provided them with more fun than stoning a stranger. Five minutes later the friends from Cold Aston came driving towards me, anxious because I had not appeared on time. When I told them what had happened one said: "Before the roads were metalled these hill-top villages rarely saw a stranger except on horseback or in a carriage. Any stranger on foot who wasn't a pedlar or tradesman would be looked upon with suspicion."

"And not so long before that in Saxon times one would have had to blow a horn on entering a village to show one came with no evil intent," I retorted, still sore at the miserable encounter.

I doubt if this would happen at Notgrove or any other village today. With better roads and easier transport the isolation of the countryside has come to an end and the childrens' horizons are no longer bounded by the few miles around their homes. The older ones go to school in the nearest big centre travelling by school bus and most of them when not watching television are more likely to be playing spacemen than the primitive hunt-the-stranger game.

On some maps Cold Aston is named Aston Blank, "Cold" and "Blank" having the same meaning. The village is open to wind and weather and for nine months and often twelve months of the year Cold Aston describes it well, though I expect its inhabitants grow tired of jokes about its name. They do affirm, however, that it is one of the healthiest places on Cotswold, and the air is certainly exhilarating, so exhilarating that it rarely tempts one to linger. It would be easy to walk through it to the open wolds and not be aware of several charming old houses, sensibly built long and low, hidden behind the sheltering walls and shrubs of their gardens.

We used to confuse it with Cold Ashton because of an error in the Gloucestershire *Highways and Byways*, our cherished guide to the Cotswolds, and wilfully, I am afraid, we refused to accept the truth that Cold Ashton was a village in the south-west corner of the region near Bath. This was because one summer when we were staying near Northleach one of our special walks was to Salperton and back across the wolds. The morning walk along the ridgeway to Salperton and the happy time spent there with friends was always a delight, but by the time we reached Cold Aston on the way home we were tired and hungry and to keep our feet and fatigue under control we used to march the last few miles quietly singing the old song:

> Ride! Ride! with red spur there is death in delay
> 'Tis a race for dear life with the devil;

If dark Cromwell prevail and the King must give way
This earth is no place for Sir Bevil.

This song is quoted in *Highways and Byways* to illustrate the story of Sir Bevil Grenville, the cavalier, who died in the old rectory at Cold Ashton after the Battle of Lansdown in 1643. Being passionate royalists and of an age to believe that death in battle was more noble than living to fight another day, this battle, where only 600 out of some 2,000 cavaliers survived, stirred our imaginations in a way that the Battle of Stow with its surrender to the Cromwellians by Sir Jacob Astley never did.

Cold Aston has no grey gabled Tudor mansion like Cold Ashton in the south, and its church of St. Andrew of Norman origin was badly restored in 1875. The remains of a stone reredos with a canopied niche, the ornate but much battered Easter Sepulchre can still be seen with a few fragments of Norman moulding.

Lower Slaughter lies about a half mile west of the Foss Way and some two miles north-west of Bourton on the Water, and is much more picturesque than the hill villages and more widely known. This popularity has been a mixed blessing. It has become a little Bourton on the Water to coach passengers on a tour of the Cotswolds and resembles it in having a clear sparkling stream intersected by little bridges as its main attraction. There are also some charming old stone cottages on one side of the stream if one is fortunate to see them without parked cars spoiling the picture. They might serve as illustrations to those sentimental ballads sung in Victorian times in many a town parlour whose windows looked out on the grimy aftermath of the Industrial Revolution, ballads where roses bloomed eternally round cottage doors and life was a cycle of rural felicity and homely beauty.

Upper Slaughter has a closer affinity with the hills and it is from the high country to the north I like to come to it. Less obviously picturesque than Lower Slaughter its more complex pattern is determined by the steep narrow-sided valley of the Ey and the curving Slaughter Brook spanned by a little bridge linking houses half way up a bank with farm buildings and cottages on the other side. In summer great dragonflies dart and flicker about the willow herb and meadow-sweet lining the brook, and pied and

Lower Slaughter: (above) old village houses,
and (below) new—but in traditional style

yellow wagtails walk delicately in and out of the shallow water or flirt their tails on the walls, a bird adornment whose subtle colouring suits the old grey stone perfectly.

Upper Slaughter also possesses a twelve-gabled Elizabethan manor house with a two-storeyed Jacobean porch which is not only one of the architectural treasures of the Cotswolds but a good example of how time has mellowed the later addition of the porch into harmony with the whole building. I like to look at the manor house from a field gate on the road to Lower Slaughter on a sunny day when the stone gleams silvery grey against the dark wooded heights of Stow and Maugersbury. On an overcast day the stone takes on the colour of the shadowed sky making its walls seem unsubstantial and the whole building withdrawn.

The village of Lower Swell is just over a mile west of Stow on the Wold. Both Upper and Lower Swell are riverside villages of the Dikler valley, between the high ridge where the lonely village of Condicote stands and the hill holding Stow on its summit. The old jingle "All the way from Swell to Stow a squirrel can hop without wetting his toe", is still true of both villages if the squirrel could manage a few particularly long hops for the first fifty yards or so, for both the Cheltenham road leading to Lower Swell and the Tewkesbury road leading to Upper Swell from Stow are tree-fringed with a lilting dip and rise as they go along.

There are the remains of five long barrows in the Swell region and the Royce collection contains hundreds of flint arrowheads found there. Flint is not present in oolitic limestone and worked or unworked must have been brought from the chalk downs on the other side of the Thames, the nearest source, or from the east of England. Springs gush out from many places on the hillside and I find it easy to believe the theory that the neolithic people who raised the long barrows worshipped running water and this was one reason for the close concentration of their burial mounds here. The striking contrast with the bare waterless wolds must have made the springs givers of life and bounty.

There is evidence of Bronze Age barrows also, one actually in the churchyard, and traces of a Roman burial ground have also been found here. These ancient dead cast no melancholy over Lower Swell today for it is one of the most open of Cotswold villages and its clear stream bordered by the wild flowers whose

10

Eighteenth-century façade at Lower Swell

roots love running water make it a pleasant place in which to linger on a summer day when the hills are parched under a scorching sun.

Upper Swell lies a mile north-west and the Dikler makes its own way between the villages, first passing Bowl Farm, once the home of Sir Robert Atkyns the county historian, and then being captured to make a water garden in the grounds of Abbotwood. Coming to the village from Stow it begins with a stone bridge over the river and a mill, and then the houses and cottages grouped about the manor house and tiny church which still keeps a Norman south doorway to remind us of its earliest foundation. It is a more compact village than Lower Swell, and the manor house of late Tudor and Stuart times, a beautiful example of the English Renaissance, gives it a special grace. The manor house is not shut away behind a high wall or hidden by trees. It is part of the village street and loses neither dignity nor beauty by this, gaining by contrast with the more homely dwellings on each side and seeming to watch over the village with a well-mannered acceptance of its age-old position and receiving the same from it.

The A44 from Oxfordshire crosses the Foss Way at the southern end of Moreton in Marsh and begins a slow climb to high country and then along the Five Mile Drive to Broadway where it leaves Cotswold in an abrupt fall to the Vale of Evesham. About half a mile from Moreton the A44 passes on the left a tree-shaded drive leading to Sezincote, that domed house in a "Hindu" setting of lakes, garden temples, little bridges decorated with elephants, sacred bulls and such-like eastern conceits, built by Sir Charles Cockerell of the East India Company on his return from India in the early nineteenth century. Repton helped with the designs and it is thought that many of them were influenced by plates in Daniel's *Oriental Scenery*. It is possible, also, that Repton was glad to experiment in oriental styles in preparation for designing the Brighton Pavilion which he built soon after for the Prince Regent.

The first time I went to Sezincote some thirty years ago on a summer evening I had not been told anything about the house and expected to see a mellow Cotswold mansion of the traditional kind. A mist from the lake caught in a light breeze moved in slow coils and streamers over the park and when I was being shown the grounds I began to wonder if the tot of elderberry wine I had been given before setting out had been too potent and I was in the grip of some horrid form of intoxication which combined with the mist was affecting my vision.

My kindly hostess sensing my bewilderment and probably accustomed to the reactions of new guests then gave me a short history of the house. She sounded a little apologetic, and I remember painfully even now how brash and condescending I must have sounded when I told her that although traditional styles are best suited to the region an occasional excursion into the exotic could give a certain piquancy to the scene and that after all it is people who live in a place who make it interesting. But in those days I had not learned that the Cotswolds has a way of absorbing eccentricities and that a house not in the vernacular could have its place. Moreover eccentricity has always been part of the English character and the English scene. As Sterne puts it in his *Sentimental Journey*, "One can see the precise and distinguishing marks of national character more in these nonsensical minutiae than in the most important matters of state."

The Brighton Pavilion as an architectural achievement is an improvement on Sezincote, but Sezincote scores because of its situation on a broad sloping hillside surrounded by parkland where cedars and other foreign trees have grown to a mature and splendid beauty, and where a willow-hung lake provides a haven for native water-fowl.

Sezincote was once a sizable parish with its own church. According to ancient documents as far back as 1086 it found employment for twelve teams, but like many other villages it shrank with the coming of the Enclosures. In 1638 its church was in ruins and in 1751 the benefice was amalgamated with Longborough. Now it consists of a big house, a stud farm and farm cottages.

Once the A44 has passed the entrance to Batsford Park and its woods on the opposite side of the road to Sezincote the hill begins to steepen as it comes to Bourton on the Hill, a tiny village flanking the road just before it reaches the summit. The old cottages cling to the hillside with dry-stone walls to keep the gardens from slipping into the road and to set off their flowers. From spring to autumn aubretia and other rock plants tumble over the walls flowering with a brilliance of colour Moreton gardens with their clay soil rarely attain. There is no mistaking the fact that one is back again in limestone country, and quarry country as well. The hutments, wire and concrete of a war-time station which ruined the skyline at the summit have now been cleared away and once more the wide hill-top prospect flows as far as the eye can see.

Bourton House, at the beginning of the village with its old dove-cot and fine barn, has associations with Sir Thomas Overbury whose murder by slow poisoning in the Tower of London was one of the great court scandals of James I's reign. Another Sir Thomas Overbury, nephew of the murdered man, made known to the world the mystery known as "The Campden Wonder".

The first Sir Thomas was friend and adviser to Robert Carr, first favourite of the king, but when the wife of the Earl of Essex wanted to marry Carr Sir Thomas strongly opposed the marriage, thus infuriating the lady who at once set about planning to get rid of him. Carr depended on Sir Thomas Overbury's knowledge of foreign and home affairs and at first was reluctant to help but finally he used his great influence over the king to get Sir Thomas imprisoned in the Tower, and then with Lady Essex proceeded to poison him. The poisons listed at the trial by the apothecary's apprentice included mercury, powder of diamonds, aqua fortis and spiders, and were administered in confectionery and sweetmeats sent by the lady ostensibly to sweeten the diet of his confinement.

It took three years for Sir Thomas to die and a few days later Lady Essex obtained her divorce. Three months after she was married to Carr, the wedding being attended by the king and celebrated in extravagant style with all the pomp and show the court could devise. The king heaped even more favours on his favourite and made him Earl of Somerset, thus making him more enemies he could not control without the experienced aid of his old friend Sir Thomas Overbury.

It was inevitable that the murder would out. The apothecary talked and Carr's enemies made full use of this confession to uncover the whole horrid plot. Intrigue, spite, corruption of all kinds were commonplace in James's court but murder by slow poison could not be tolerated once it became widely known. Carr and his wife with their four accomplices were arrested but only the four accomplices were hanged, Carr and his lady being confined to the

Tower for five years and then pardoned. Meanwhile a new favourite, the handsome young George Villiers, had taken his place, being rapidly raised through every rank of the peerage to become Duke of Buckingham. When Carr was released he was never allowed to regain his old position, cast-off favourites like cast-off mistresses being an embarrassment at court.

The other Sir Thomas Overbury who lived in the manor house at Bourton on the Hill was a man of letters like his uncle, but perhaps influenced by his uncle's tragic death he preferred life in the country to life at court. He was keenly interested in religious affairs. His pamphlet *Queries proposed to the Serious Consideration of those who impose upon others in Things Divine and Supernatural Revelation and Persecute any upon the account of Religion* has disappeared, but an answer to it, also with a very long title, in a booklet by George Vernon, vicar of Bourton on the Hill, published in 1677, is available. *Ataxaie Obstaculum, and Answer to certaine Queries dispersed in some parts of Gloucestershire* makes dusty reading today except to students of such matters, though while marvelling at the literary pursuits of a clergyman of a small rural parish one must remember the deep concern felt by everyone in religious matters in those days, for they could bring degradation, ruin and even death. I imagine that the vicar and Sir Thomas Overbury had many an interesting argument to enliven winter evenings at Bourton.

Sir Thomas Overbury was also the author of the first account of the Campden Wonder, an event which made as much stir at the time throughout England as the murder of his uncle, and probably excited the local people much more. Briefly it tells of William Harrison, seventy years old and of sober respectable habit, steward to Juliana, Lady Campden, who disappeared when collecting rents a few miles from home, and of Joan Perry and her two sons John and Richard, who were hung for his murder on the confession of John, who was Harrison's servant. A year and a half later Harrison returned home with a strange story of having been kidnapped and sold into slavery in Turkey. Soon after his return his wife committed suicide. Manuscript notes in Anthony Wood's copy of Overbury's pamphlet describe her as being "a snotty, covetuous Presbyterian".

Andrew Lang, John Masefield and Hugh Ross Williamson were

all fascinated by the story. Masefield turned it into a play and Hugh Ross Williamson into a novel. In *The Campden Wonder*, a study of the story edited by Sir John Clark and published by the Oxford University Press in 1959, all the available particulars and theories from the original by Sir Thomas Overbury onward are set out, but the mystery still remains. It does cast light, however, on the twisted mind of John Perry, who confessed to a murder he had not committed and who also implicated his mother and brother. New evidence, the finding of the Campden Grammar School account books a few years ago, reveals that the signatures of Harrison, who was one of the foefees, are missing for the three years between the relevant dates. When they ceased it was probably because he was dead or had resigned because of extreme old age.

It is interesting that Sir Thomas Overbury was also a foefee whose name appears many times in the account book with Harrison's. Sir George Clark suggests this may be significant. As Sir Thomas has been "a great traveller beyond the seas in his early days it does seem likely that he might have provided the material for Harrison's incredible story of being a slave in Smyrna".

The heart of the mystery is why did Harrison disappear and where did he go? Sir John Clark's book gives sufficient reasons to explain the behaviour of John Perry. The puzzle grows more fascinating as one attempts to sort out fact from fiction; it combines so many familiar ingredients of story-telling common to the period.

Joan Perry was reputed to be a witch and was hanged first so that her two sons could be released from her spells and thus confess, which they would not do, John Perry declaring with his last breath that his master would return again and that he had lied in saying they had killed him. Superstition has its place, for when Richard Perry met his two children on the way to church under guard "both their noses fell a bleeding, which was looked upon as ominous", and a romantic element which might have come out of the *Arabian Nights* creeps in when Harrison tells how he was employed to concoct medicines from herbs for his master, an ancient physician, and returned home by the aid of a silver bowl, a gift from his master.

There is, of course, a more prosaic conclusion that it was necessary for political reasons concerning some very important people why William Harrison should be hidden during the upheaval just before and after the Restoration: as Lady Juliana and her family were Royalists this does not make sense.

Not one story at all, but several, all mixed together and served with plenty of local colour to give it the semblance of authenticity. I feel much inclined to suspect Sir Thomas Overbury of being a forerunner of Defoe, who made Robinson Crusoe's adventures so real that it is hard to believe he never visited that lonely island.

XIV

CHELTENHAM

CHELTENHAM'S claim to be considered a Cotswold town does not lie in its architecture and lay-out. Farming was its chief concern from the Middle Ages to the middle of the eighteenth century, and the wool merchants and clothiers who enriched most Cotswold towns during that period played little part in its growth and economy. In the thirteenth century Henry III sold the manor to the Norman Benedictine abbey of Fecamp in exchange for land in Winchelsea and Rye which was of more strategic importance to him in his recurring quarrels with France, so that it was never dominated by a particular family or resident landlord and no great castle or house was built there.

In the earliest Worcester cartulary its charter is grouped under Winchcombshire along with Beckford, Bishop's Cleeve, Andoversford, Withington, Notgrove and Aston Blank, and like other towns of Gloucestershire it probably owed its growth as a market town to the fact it was on the high road between Gloucester and Winchcombe. It appears in the tax-list of 1307 as an urban community, and in 1311 as a borough. Leland describes it as a small market town, with buildings of brick and thatch, and so it might have continued if a chance discovery of its special waters in 1761 had not turned it into a spa. Its architectural flowering began soon after and continued until the middle of the nineteenth century.

It grew in snowball fashion out of the desire of the nobility and gentry for an agreeable place in which to spend their time while taking the medicinal waters and baths prescribed by the fashionable doctors of the period, and because a few far-sighted men watching the development of Bath realized this would be good business for themselves and for the town.

Cobbett, with his characteristic gusty bludgeoning called it one of the devouring "wens", a place where "East India plunderers, West India floggers, English tax-gorgers, together with gluttons, drunkards and debauchees of all descriptions . . . at the suggestion of silently laughing quacks, in the hope of getting rid of the bodily consequences of their manifold sins and iniquities." The Cheltenham people burned his effigy and would have done his person harm when he came to give a political lecture in the town if he had not managed to escape to Stow, whose inhabitants were less urban-minded and more in sympathy with his ideas.

The market recorded by Leland, and the town's other expansion through the centuries as a shopping centre for the farms and villages for miles around was the chief reason why Cheltenham became part of Cotswold life as well as a watering-place for invalids and other visitors. Later it developed into an entertainment, cultural and education centre, and the countryman still finds there a taste of town life with a metropolitan rather than a provincial flavour. In return country neighbours from the wolds bring to Cheltenham a more robust and brisk atmosphere. Although your true Cotsaller has a reputation for reserve this tends to relax in the bustle of town. Or do they subconsciously feel that their way of life is more vital than the ways of the somewhat subdued and well-mannered townsfolk? I have noticed, particularly out of the tourist season, how a group of country people shopping, lunching, or gossiping in and around the High Street and Promenade can enliven the place.

The climate is gentler than that of the uplands where the wind blows cold for nine months or more of the year. Protected on the north and east by the steep limestone escarpment, it lies open on the south and west to the kinder airs of the Severn plain, mitigating the harshness of spring and in summer producing an almost languorous atmosphere, while winter's rigours are tempered by the high sheltering wall of the hills. The climate is one of the reasons why the town became for many years a place of retirement for the Anglo-Indians, incidentally providing types of retired military men and civil servants of the Empire on which the humorists of the time could exercise their skill.

Looking down on the town from Cleeve Cloud its spires and clustering buildings compose themselves into an inviting picture, and though most valley towns take on a disarming quality, a suggestion of defencelessness, when contemplated from a near-by hill-top, the realist expects this felicity to disintregrate on closer acquaintance. Cheltenham, however, does not disappoint the traveller when he descends from the hills. Despite the busyness of the streets a sense of past leisureliness and urbanity still pervades them. The austere stone façades of its Georgian houses and terraces keep a well-mannered aloofness and dignity, a little outworn and decayed but still strong enough to arouse nostalgia for a world where there was so much room in which to grow and whose planners knew exactly what they wanted and succeeded in doing it. And it is pleasant to remember that though the style is mainly that of the classic revival of the eighteenth and nineteenth centuries the stone came from quarries on Leckhampton Hill a mile or so away.

The old Leckhampton quarries are deserted now except for occasional fossil-hunters, and the rails of its tramway have disappeared. There remains, however, an isolated pinnacle of hard limestone blocks known as the Devil's Chimney behind an Iron Age promontory fort, Leckhampton Camp, on the edge of the steep cliff. To me the Devil's Chimney looks alien to the smooth rolling contours of the hills one sees stretching for miles behind Cleeve Cloud, and it is interesting that the Devil does not come into Cotswold folklore as often as it does in the legends of country nearer the Severn and the Welsh border. There are a number of standing stones on Cotswold which might easily have acquired his name, though they are the last vestiges of long barrows and not natural. Perhaps the country folk who named Devil's Chimney saw it as something that did not belong to the Cotswold scene. However, it makes an excuse, for those who need one, for a climb to the hill-top to look at the view.

Cheltenham, like Winchcombe, was a Gloucestershire tobacco town in the second half of the seventeenth century, and its fight to keep its tobacco plantations is one of the more lively stories in its history. It was one of the first places in England to grow tobacco and though the parliaments of James I and Charles II prohibited its growing and sent troops to destroy the fields it continued to defy the authorities, and its end came about as much by the cheapness of Virginian tobacco as by rigorous repression. For Winchcombe the loss of its tobacco trade meant poverty and degradation but Cheltenham did not suffer so badly. An increase in the malt trade was a small compensation, though this was only sufficient to keep it alive. If it had not been for the discovery of the medicinal springs it might have remained a small market town with poor communications, its only buildings of note St. Mary's church and the Corn and Butter Market on its stone pillars in the High Street.

These with the prison beneath them were swept away in 1786 when foot pavements were made for the comfort of those who came to take the waters. One imagines there were people in those days who deplored their passing, but it was no tearing down of the old to make way for haphazard building of the new as so often happens today; Cheltenham was entering into an era of dignified and planned expansion.

How in 1761 the waters first became known has been crystallized into one of those legends involving birds and animals founding a city which have a familiar ring. This is no place to delve into the origin of tales going back to Roman and pre-Roman times, but it seems fitting that Cheltenham, a town that owes its distinction to the Classic Revival of the eighteenth century should thus explain its beginning as a watering-place.

The first saline spring, we are told, was discovered when pigeons were noticed pecking grains of salt formed on the surface of damp ground about a spring near the River Chelt. It is likely that the humbler local inhabitants as well as the birds knew of its health-giving properties and had used it for centuries, unless it suddenly issued forth from the ground like an act of providence to start Cheltenham on its way to becoming a spa. The pigeon now has an honourable place in the town's coat of arms and this gentle if voracious bird rather than the more war-like eagle is a more seemly image for a town concerned with healing. A wag did once point out a similarity between the gait and stance of an elderly obese gentleman taking the waters and the strutting of the bird, but the days when Cheltenham provoked wits and rebels are over now, their jokes nothing but bric-a-brac mouldering in history's dusty attics.

A Mr. Mason who owned the land where the spring was found fenced it in, built a rustic thatched-roofed well-house over it, and proceeded to sell the waters. As time went by more springs were discovered in other parts of the town, though pigeons do not seem to have assisted in later discoveries. As spas were then beginning to come into fashion it is likely they were eagerly sought for by Cheltenham landowners. And so it came about that Cheltenham had several spas each with its own proprietor and set of buildings. Some of these sites are now forgotten, but the buildings of others still remain as part of the town's eighteenth-century heritage. The chief concentration finally settled in the area south of the ancient High Street and today this is still the hub of Cheltenham's baths and water-drinking, its social and shopping life.

It was Henry Skillicorne, a Bristol sea-captain, who saw the real possibilities of Cheltenham's waters. He married Mason's daughter Elizabeth and on retiring to Cheltenham to end his days it came to him that his wife's inheritance of the original spring could turn the town into a spa known beyond the locality. At first he planned a small resort such as the Bristol Hotwells in the Clifton gorge familiar to him in his Bristol days. He had many friends and wealthy patrons whom he had served well as a sea-captain and who were willing to help him. One of these, Mr. Norbonne Berkeley, later Lord Botetourt, made him a design for a long avenue of elms to enhance the new lay-out of the well-head, and this being a period when gentlemen of leisure understood the gothic adornment of the natural scene Old Well Walk rising up the lower slopes of Bayshill ended on the north with a vista of the tower and spire of the church, making a pleasant self-contained promenade for the water-drinkers.

Other patrons helped to publicize the spa, and Handel, Dr. Johnson, the Countess of Huntingdon and the poet Shenstone were visitors between 1744 and 1749. One of the Captain's minor claims to fame is that his epitaph, a potted biography as well as an eulogy, is one of the longest in an English church, even in that age of long-winded, pompous memorials.

After the Captain's death in 1763 his son and a Mr. Millar from London built the first of Cheltenham's Long Rooms for the entertainment of visitors, and a more spectacular transformation of the town began. It was now to have all the refinements including a Master of Ceremonies, terraces of new houses to lodge the visitors, paved footpaths and gas-lighting in the streets on moonless nights. In the summer of 1788 George III paid a visit to take the waters and with this royal patronage Cheltenham was all set to become the first watering-place in England.

Before this could be accomplished, however, the serious problem of the transport of stone, timber and other heavy building materials, as well as coal, in an era without railways or well-surfaced roads had to be overcome. In 1792 when the canal mania was already sweeping England a canal was planned to run from the Severn to Combe Hill, but the war years of 1793 to 1815 put an end to developments on any large scale. It was not until 1809 that an Act was passed for laying a "Gloucester and Cheltenham Rail or Tramway", an early example of horse-drawn trucks along iron rails. This tramway was opened in 1811 from a quay in Gloucester, then extended from the docks at the end of the Berkeley Ship Canal to the lower end of Cheltenham, with a branch running steeply to the quarries on Leckhampton Hill south of the town.

No time was wasted once the main transport problems were solved. The architects and builders must have learned much from Ralph Allen's rebuilding of Bath some fifty years before and the naming of one of Cheltenham's earliest Regency housing schemes as the Royal Crescent might be regarded as an acknowledgement of this. As an example of Regency domestic architecture it has elegance and dignity, the severity of its stone façade relieved by canopied balconies of ironwork.

The ornamental cast iron work of Cheltenham's Regency houses is one of the town's special attractions. Before this time ironwork had been made by individual craftsmen, and was used mainly for church furnishings, wrought iron gates, brackets for lamps and inn signs. The rapid growth of Regency houses and terraces demanded balconies, railings, verandas and porches to set off their plain façades, and these had to be produced in quantity. The answer was to obtain them from founderies and not individual craftsmen, and as an early example of mass-production should have reassured those who deplored this new progress. Unfortunately, after 1830, the ironwork became heavier until it degenerated into commonplace and depressing designs, including those hundreds of miles of dreary spear-headed railings so mercifully swept away in the big towns by the drive for iron scrap during the last world war.

Cheltenham's need for these kind of fitments coincided with the years when the iron work was at its highest peak of excellence, and though other towns such as Bath and Leamington can show a similar use of this form of industrial art, with the same designs in many cases, in Cheltenham the examples run into many hundreds and it is the diversity of the patterns as well as the number which adds so much to the charm of the terraces and villas of the town. Most of the designs are from Cottingham's Smith and Founder Director of 1813, and the ironwork came from the founderies of the Midlands brought to Cheltenham by the new canal and tramway.

With their purity of outline, the curves, circles and half circles held together without emphasis by guiding straight bars, the rigidity of the material contrasting with the flexibility of the patterns, the Grecian designs made the perfect embellishment to stone or stucco frontages which had no other adornment. The satisfaction this ironwork gives to the eye is heightened by the way the delicate outlines, like the tendrils, stems and leaves of climbing plants reduced to basic forms, are duplicated when they cast their shadows on the light-coloured walls. Today one of the best places to see it is in the short streets of smaller houses lying back from the High Street.

It was inevitable that a town built and devoted mainly to the entertainment and health of people of leisure should attract its Savonarola, Francis Close, a clergyman and a "despot of goodness", whose puritanical conscience denounced drink, racing, Popery, Sunday trains and the theatre as temptations of the devil with equal fervour. When the theatre was burnt down in 1839 he had sufficient influence to prevent its rebuilding, and it must have seemed at the time that his fanatical zeal would change the whole conception of Cheltenham. However when he became Dean Close and left the town to take up new duties and exhort a new flock the theatre was rebuilt and racing began again.

Apart from his religious influence he was mainly responsible for starting Cheltenham on the way to becoming an educational centre. This has continued to grow with the years and today there are three public schools for boys, and one for girls, the Cheltenham Ladies College, as well as technical and art schools and two Church of England training colleges for teachers, and it is not unlikely that in the future it will have its own university. The re-introduction of the Gothic style for Anglican churches was dear to his heart, and before he left he laid the foundation stone of Christ Church, no doubt praying as he did so for the end of the Greek revival with its auras of paganism and reason, and a return to the simple faith and piety expressed in medieval days by the upward pointing Gothic arch.

Fortune, it would seem, has always smiled on Cheltenham, or perhaps the town has always been alert to seize opportunity when it came. Perhaps, also, the right people have come along at the right time to direct its affairs. In one instance this certainly happened, for the Ladies College, originating in the need for high grade education for the daughters of upper middle class residents soon changed from a day school to a boarding establishment. Miss Dorothea Beale, that revered advocate of university training for women, was its headmistress, and under her leadership the reputation of the school was assured. The town could now put *"eruditic"* alongside *"salubritas"* on its motto, a book as well as a pigeon on the borough coat of arms.

Cheltenham, a town deliberately created as a setting for a cultured and civilized life of leisure still serves its original purpose, with a considerable amount of light industry to give substance and balance to its economy. With the fitness which has distinguished it from its Regency days the printing trade is one of those light industries.

XV

THE SOUTH COTSWOLDS AND THE CLOTHIERS

WHEREAS the medieval wool trade gave us the Perpendicular churches and the little grey wool towns of the north Cotswolds the most visible contribution to a portrait of the south Cotswold scene is the cloth mills of the seventeenth and eighteenth centuries centred around Stroud, Chalford, Painswick, and Wotton under Edge in the extreme south-west corner. This progression from the marketing of raw wool to the manufacture of cloth became possible in the south Cotswolds because of the beds of fuller's earth found there between the Inferior and Great Oolite absent in the north-east of the region. Fuller's earth was used for cleansing and felting the fabric, and where the fullers were established the rest of the industry, the carders, staplers, weavers and dyers had to follow. The copious springs of soft water gushing out of the steep-sided valleys were also a necessity to the industry.

The trade shaped the life and the houses of the majority of the people. It produced clothiers to take the place of wool-men as the most important merchants in the country. Some became Gentlemen Clothiers buying country estates from their profits and building new mansions or taking over the old manor houses and so continuing to influence local affairs as lords of the manor when they had given up trade. Their sons and grandsons married into the peerage or received honours in their own right because of their status, while others less fortunate or less astute, particularly those who came in at the end of the eighteenth century, were ruined when the boom was over. In consequence hundreds of their workers also suffered or moved from the district to find work elsewhere. And except for Stroud, which partially adopted the use of steam as well as water power after 1830, and which continued to grow into a factory town with the usual sprawl and litter of late nineteenth century industrialism, the region lost little of its Cotswold charm.

The complex make-up of the landscape with its rounded buffs,

Uley Bury

high plateaux and deep ravines was on a large enough scale to
dwarf the factories and mills and keep them from spoiling the
scene. Placed in the narrow valleys they became accessories in the
wide panorama rather than focal points.

The villages with cottages clinging to the terraced slopes and
interlaced with tortuous lanes have their own dramatic qualities,
the stone shining out on the open hillsides and flanked with hanging woods of beech, ash and conifers.

When the manufacture first began to emerge on a commercial
scale about 1450 it was a rural industry and so it continued for
nearly three hundred years. Under the domestic system agriculture and industry went on side by side. Before the Enclosures the
cottage weaver, though he worked long hours, and very often
his family as well, had a plot of land for vegetables and could keep
a cow, hens, geese and even a few sheep on the common land to
supplement his poor pay, while by carrying on business in a
country district the early cloth manufacturers and merchants
escaped municipal and gild regulations, the gild system with its
rigid rules about quality and quantity each member was allowed
to produce not being favourable to the free enterprise of this new
class of capitalists.

Many of the cottages one sees today having a larger floor space
and wider windows than average belong to the time when weaving was done in the workers' homes and good light as well as
space for the looms was required. The weavers' cottages were
usually sprinkled on the hillsides not far from the springs and
streams where the yarn could be washed, and this explains why so
many of the clothing villages do not fall into the usual village
pattern either of a community gathered round the church and
manor house or strung out along a road.

Chalford, in the Golden Valley, is a good example of this. The
cottages are mainly set out on the terraced side of the valley, dotted here and there in haphazard clusters on different levels and
served by little roads, once packhorse lanes, twisting up the slopes
and growing steeper the higher they climb. Memoirs and journals
of the period vividly describe how when coach and carriage
transport came into fashion with the rising fortunes of the clothiers
these lanes caused much trouble to horses and coachmen in bad
weather.

11

Village in South Cotswold

Seen from the opposite side of the river far enough away to bring the whole hill-face into view Chalford and Bisley can look very attractive. The aptness of Bigland's "a very Alpine hamlet" suggests that he, also, must have viewed Chalford from such a position. Indeed, it is difficult to get a comprehensive picture of Chalford or Bisley in any other way.

It was not until the eighteenth century that mills to house looms driven by water power were erected in the valley bottoms with terraces of houses for the workers. How many who witnessed this beginning of factory life realized the way it would develop in the north of England when the coming of steam power caused the bulk of the trade to be concentrated there. Anyone who has seen the rows after rows of small brick dwellings packed together in monotonous repetition, grimed with the smoke of factory chimneys, with asphalted yards instead of gardens, where grace and natural living have little place, can rejoice that the Golden Valley escaped this fate.

It had mills in plenty, the bottom of the deeply-cleft hillside being so narrow that there was room for little else beside the river, the canal and the road. Strongly and squarely built of dressed blocks of local stone, which has a silvery gleam rather than the creamy yellow of north Cotswold oolite they give the area a distinction unique on Cotswold, where the tendency is for buildings to merge into the background. In some moods one might see them as industry in its pleasantest form before it became translated into the ugliness of the Industrial Revolution. The internal history of the trade does not altogether fit in with this idyllic picture.

One of the dubious benefits of the Stroudwater Canal was the bringing of Welsh slates to the district and in many cases they have supplanted the original stone tiles; alien in colour and texture they add a certain starkness to the overall effect. But here again the stone provides a harmonizing link, as if the masons could not forbear adding those special touches to soften the gaunt tall blocks and bring them into relationship with the Cotswold vernacular. In many instances the octagonal or square chimneys are gracefully designed, and as no Cotswold mason could resist the influence of the late Perpendicular gothic the mill windows are often reminiscent of the seventeenth-century Cotswold style. Most of the mills we see today are of four or five storeys and belong to the early nineteenth century; the earlier ones were lower, expanding outward when more space was needed. As the trade increased this was no longer possible in the restricted valley bottom.

In St. Mary's House Chalford has at least one house belonging to a mill-owner conscious of the new Renaissance sweeping the country. Originally it was a simple, flat-fronted dwelling, but sash windows, balustrades and a beautiful shell-headed doorway transformed it into a Gentleman Clothier's residence.

A number of the clothiers had already become Gentlemen Clothiers and were amongst the wealthiest men on Cotswold by the time Sir Robert Atkyn retired to his house at Pinbury Park near Sapperton to complete his *History of Gloucestershire*. "The clothing trade is so eminent in this county that no other manufacture deserves a mention," he wrote in 1712.

Josiah Tucker, Dean of Gloucester, depicts a clothier and the way he conducted his business. "One person, with a great stock and large credit, buys the wool, pays for the Spinning, Weaving, Milling, Shearing, Dressing etc. That is, he is master of the whole manufacture from first to last, and probably employs a thousand persons under him."

It can be seen from this how easy it was for a clothier to become all-powerful in his own district. Josiah Tucker wanted him to remain so, being one of those clerics who considered it his duty to castigate workers seeking better wages and conditions. He was one of those clerics, also, who must have been a great asset to the Free Churches of the day by sending the people to the chapels instead of to church for comfort and understanding. "Such brutality and Ignorance, such Debauchery and Extravagance, such Idleness, Irreligion, Cursing and Swearing and contempt for all rule and authority human and divine, do not reign so triumphantly among the Poor in any other country as in ours."

Though some of these epithets might apply to weavers and others employed in the cloth trade whose conditions were so wretched that they sought any means to forget them, the word "extravagance" shows what little feeling the Dean had for the humbler people of his diocese. The intransigent poor was one of his favourite subjects. On another occasion he wrote: "How absurd must every project be for securing or increasing this trade which does not tend to secure or increase the diligence and frugality of the people."

True, the last quotation comes from material written at a time when an overloaded market was making things difficult for the Gentlemen Clothiers, but one wonders at the blindness of any man who could preach frugality to weavers whose wages were barely above starvation level.

Local wool was used in making worsteds for the East India Company, who were the chief customers for the mills of the valley, though by the time the company was established the famous long-fleeced Cotswold breed of sheep had been crossed with Leicestershires to provide a coarser wool. Indeed, the supply of local wool was insufficient to meet the demand. It was estimated that by the middle of the eighteenth century Stroud alone needed between two and three million fleeces a year, and wool had to be brought from other sheep-rearing districts as well as the Cotswolds.

William Ireland, a clothier of Chalford, made a stout heavy cloth from wool from the Forest of Dean; others obtained wool from Hereford, Leominster and Ross, and even went as far afield as Kent for their supply. There must have been a constant creaking and pounding of wagon wheels on the little roads diverging into the valley and one can see today how deeply they were eaten into the hillsides. Not only the pack-horses and ponies and the wagons but the steepness of the gradients which turned them into water-courses during heavy rain helped to scour them into deep channels between high banks before their surfaces were metalled. These winding roads are characteristic of the region, and while they have their hazards for the motorist and the walker shade, shelter and unexpected vistas often compensate for the stiff climb.

Spanish merino wool was already being imported into the district, but though soft and easily worked it was not generally used for nearly a hundred years after its first introduction at the end of the sixteenth century. It only became popular when George III obtained a flock of merino sheep which he gave into the care of Sir Joseph Banks. It was not long before Sir Joseph was telling the king that demand for the sheep was rapidly increasing, especially in Gloucestershire.

Edward Shepperd, who built Gatcombe Park near Avening and

was one of the most important clothiers on Cotswold, crossed the Spanish merino sheep with his Ryelands giving as one reason the necessity of being prepared in case relations with Spain were broken off, though the more urgent reason was probably cheapness and economy, the need, as he put it for "counteracting the spirit of monopoly which prevails in the trade", a remark which has a familiar ring today.

As time went on the Spanish Merino was superseded by wool from Germany. Playnes' of Avening were the first to introduce it in 1818. K. G. Ponting in an article on the wool trade in a journal of the Textile Institute tells how in 1824 William Playne made his first expedition to Germany to buy wool himself from the great estates, driving from Calais across Europe to Breslau and Dresden. It was not long before it became an annual practice to make journeys to Germany for wool-buying, which makes one remember that in the Middle Ages the Cotswold merchants went to the Low Countries to sell not buy wool. Being of a finer quality the German wool soon took first place in the manufacture of fine cloth, with Cotswold wool used only for the coarser kinds.

It was about 1850 when Australian wool reached the Stroud valley mills. "There is a great kindness in the wool," wrote one of the merchants, and going through the available correspondence of the clothing firms of the nineteenth century many a pregnant phrase and word makes one realize how commercial correspondence has deteriorated into jargon in the last 150 years, though it must be confessed the spelling is often erratic.

The mills of the Stroud valley specialized in the production of fine cloth. They made the red cloth for Army uniforms, the water of the River Frome being suitable for the production of a clear scarlet dye. Stretched out on tenterhooks to dry on Rank Hill the days when a scarlet hillside blossomed among the soft greys and greens of the Cotswold uplands must have been one of the sights of the neighbourhood.

The cloth was sold by factors or middlemen who operated in the London and Bristol markets. Incidentally, there were many complaints against the factors by the manufacturers, complaints still common today. Often they became richer and more powerful than the men who supplied the goods, "by insensible degrees" attaining "the power of the principal yet still preserving the appearance, the indemnity and every other advantage of the agent" as one writer of the period puts it. But it was impossible to do without factors as the export trade expanded and a good one with expert knowledge of overseas as well as home markets was worth his commission.

The letters of Daniel Packer, a Painswick clothier, make it plain how he relied upon his factor for advice about the kind of cloth in demand and the best places to sell it. As it moved to its greatest period of production on Cotswold the trade, as Samuel Rudder wrote, was "governed by fancy and fashion". Although the main trade was with India House, the Levant, Russia, Portugal and America the home market provided an important part of a clothier's income, particularly when war interrupted business abroad.

The manufacturers who used their imaginations and were a jump ahead of the fashion secured the buyers in the home market, for by now the new middle classes were feeling the excitement of progress in a period of expanding overseas trade when exotic goods from the East and other countries were being brought into England. People were no longer content with the old styles and fashions in cloth as in other commodities. The "superfines, seconds, forests, drabs, naps, duffils, to be found in a well-stored draper's shop" had to be of an ever-changing variety. In their turn the dyers also had to be adventurous in their colour ranges. We are apt to smile today at the fancy names given to colours by the drapery trade but this is no new way of tempting the customer. "Rich French Grey, Light Reddish Mouse, Pompadore Mix, Rich Corbeau, Plump Crimson, Olive and Eye White," to quote only a few listed in a dyeing-book from a works at Kings Stanley show that the dyers also were aware of the fashionable trend for novelty.

The climax of the Gentleman Clothier's prosperity had been reached at the end of the eighteenth century. It was about then Timothy Exell, the Gloucestershire weaver, wrote of them as "rich and opulent men; they were not only worth their thousands but their tens of thousands and their scores of tens of thousands". Some saw the red light ahead and left the industry to begin a new life as country gentlemen working their estates, others continued hoping times would never change and they would always find markets for their cloth, not realizing they had now competitors abroad as well as at home.

As the nineteenth century came in they began to discover it was not enough to produce the cloth but necessary to persuade others to buy it. The numbers of clothiers had increased also, men who came in when they saw how much money was being made and did not understand how the conditions in world markets were changing, as well as the competition from the more up-to-date mills of the north of England. Instead of getting the cloth sold as soon as it was finished it had to be stored, often for considerable periods and a letter from a neighbour to Robert Clarke Paul, a connection of the famous Paul family of Woodchester but one who does not seem to have been experienced in the trade, gives a glimpse of some of the hazards. "You had better have the cloths hung out some fine day and then paper them up close, and bond them well and you will have nothing to fear from moths and spiders."

After 1830 records show a decline in population in all the towns and villages of the south and south-west Cotswolds except Stroud. The heyday of the clothiers was over. The main trade moved to the north of England where manufacturers were busy putting up large factories and mills in which steam power was used and cloth could be turned out more cheaply.

In Painswick the expansion of the clothing trade was stimulated by a colony of Flemish weavers who settled there in the sixteenth century. The town was in at the beginning of cloth manufacture, for the spinning of yarn and the making of cloth for stockings is known to have flourished there in the early fifteenth century.

In the lord of the manor's Rent Roll for 1498 eight mills where cloth was finished and cleaned are recorded. Painswick continued to grow from that time onward until like the rest of the south Cotswold region it came to the peak of prosperity in 1830, when Lipson's Wool Industry records thirty cloth mills in the parish. The size and character of the houses in the Classical style confirms this, as do the numerous handsome box tombs to the Lovedays, Tocknells, Pallings, Pooles, Baylisses, Coxes and many another clothing family in the yew-shaded churchyard. These families, if they never achieved the social status of the Shepperds of

Gatcombe Park or the Pauls of Woodchester were men of substance who lived in considerable comfort and affluence.

Picturesque traces of Painswick's medieval life can still be seen
in the cottages of time-encrusted stone in the little streets leading
down to the stream. The main part of the town seems to have
become crystallized in the last wave of the trade's prosperity. Few
houses of any interest went up as the nineteenth century advanced
and Painswick slowly settled into a rural existence, with much
poverty amongst the humbler workers and the accompaniment
of degrading Poor Laws and Parish Relief. Like Northleach and
Burford, but not to such an extent, it revived a little in the coaching era, but this only lasted until the coming of the railways. It
then retired into rural isolation.

It was discovered by tourists when motoring first became
popular and lived genteelly on its past, and as through all its
viccisitudes after it lost its clothing trade it had never degenerated into dilapidation and makeshift this brought in a modest
return. The new motoring age of the last ten years or so has not
been so kind to that part of Painswick which lies on the A46, but
it has a group of new houses in the Cotswold style which are an
example to any modern builder in stone.

XVI

MINCHINHAMPTON

MINCHINHAMPTON derived the first part of its name from Monachyn when Hampton was held by the Abbess of Caen after the Conquest, a prefix lending itself to the alliteration of the old jingle

> Beggarly Bisley, Strutting Stroud,
> Mincing Hampton and Painswick Proud

long after the Abbess and the Normans were forgotten. She still held the town in 1369 when it acquired a market and a fair. The Market Hall in the High Street, now pleasantly restored and keeping some of its original timbers as well as a toll-board amusing to visitors because of the antiquated items of its charges, was built much later in 1698. Between these dates it grew into a small town occupied mainly with agriculture and sheep-rearing and serving the neighbourhood as a market, expanding as the cloth trade of the south Cotswolds developed into a thriving industry.

Today it is a grey sedate little town not altogether Cotswold in appearance on its outskirts but having a domestic comeliness particularly about the Market Square where there is as fascinating a collection of roofs tiled with old stone slates as to be found anywhere on the Cotswolds. Its past can be traced from what it has become rather than from visible evidence of antiquity. During the time it existed as a clothing town it was an important place. Defoe, in his *Tour Through England and Wales* produced about 1724 gives Minchinhampton with Tetbury, Cirencester, Marshfield and Fairford as one of the chief cloth towns of south Gloucestershire. Tetbury and Cirencester changed their economy when the cloth trade moved to the north of England. Minchinhampton was less or more fortunate, according to the way one looks at it, and settled into a quiet rural existence without any large industry to give it new life.

The majority of the clothiers of Minchinhampton were not wealthy merchants who bought themselves estates and became translated into country gentlemen but smaller tradesmen who found it difficult to keep afloat when large capital reserves were needed to tide them over the known crises of 1756, 1803 and 1828, as well as the smaller ones of the late eighteenth century. It did have one family, the Shepperds of Gatcombe Park, who dominated the clothing trade in the district until they, also, fell victims to the trade's dispersal to the north of England, but the history of the Shepperds would take a book to itself.

The clothiers' letters and other documents of the time available in the Gloucestershire Records Office show that many of them dropped out of the business because they could not pay their creditors. In some cases their letters tell tragic stories.

"We shall have fewer Clothiers another year. I hear there was one sent to Gloster Jail Thursday last. And last Tuesday John Haines, brother to Mr. Danial Haines shot himself in the head; he was deeply in debt for wool. . . ."

A letter from one of the creditors of Thomas Cockle of Minchinhampton, who died in debt, shows a diffidence as well as anxiety about his money, and brings the writer and the world he lived in vividly before us:

". . . . respecting the debt the late Mr. Cockle owed me which you were so obliging as to say you would pay me only last Gloster Fair day which I suppose slipped your memory being rather busy on that day had not time to seek you therefore shall esteem it a favour if you will remit me a check on your Banker or you may send it by Arnold the Cirencester carrier. . . ."

One of the very few letters expressing sympathy for a ruined clothier's family is dated 21st March, 1813. Perhaps the writer was also a father of a family. "What the children will do I know not—the wife, I suppose, may be able to work as heretofore, but not to sufficient effect to support her family."

It may be there were too many clothiers in the town struggling to build successful businesses, and even in the boom years Minchinhampton never became as wealthy as Painswick or Chalford. This may explain the truncated spire of the cruciform church of the Holy Trinity. Dr. Richard Parsons who travelled much in the early eighteenth century making notes about the various little

Cotswold towns and villages records how the upper part of the spire, being seriously decayed, was taken down. It is significant that no wealthy clothier came forward to pay for the spire's complete rebuilding; in the way that time mends all one would not have it otherwise today because it has become a characteristic feature of the town.

The church has some interesting brasses. One to Edward Halyday, who died in 1519, shows him in a fur-trimmed mantle and displays his merchant's mark. When the brass was relaid on a wall the mark was placed upside-down, which would not have pleased the wool-man, for his mark was more important to his business than his name. Another brass has effigies of John Hampton and his wife Elyn in shrouds, with their nine children, the shrouds being transparent and tied in a bunch at the head and feet.

Two smaller antiquities missing after the restoration of 1842 have since been recovered, the fourteenth-century font from a garden where it had been used as a flower pot and the old Sanctus Bell bearing the inscription "Dame Alys Hampton 1515" found in 1921 in Longford's Mill. I could find nobody to tell me how it came to be at the mill, though when it was first discovered speculations ranged from supernatural agencies to greed. Whoever removed it could have had little gratitude to Dame Alice, for it was she who gave the Common to the town as an open space for ever.

Her ghost does not seem to have frightened away the vandals who removed it in the same way as the lady of Frocester's old parish church, abandoned after a disastrous fire destroyed the half-timbered and thatched cottages around it, and the village moved a mile or so away to higher ground. Being of stone the church survived, and the bell-ringers of Coaley, a nearby village, planned to steal the bell known to have been of a very pleasant tone. One dark night they crept across the fields, climbed the tower and carried it halfway down leaving it on a landing while they went into the churchyard for a rest and a drink.

Returning to finish the job they found a little old lady sitting on top of the bell, who took no heed of them when they asked her to get off. After begging her politely several times and receiving no reply, for the old lady seemed quite unaware of them, they decided to carry her as well, for she was a slight fragile figure. But try as they would they now found it impossible to move the bell. They heaved and tugged and sweated with no result. Slowly it dawned on them she was not a creature of this world at all. Doubtless an owl hooted derisively and the terror that lives by night in a lonely churchyard seized them for they turned and fled home as fast as they could, leaving the bell behind. It was later that someone remembered it was a woman who had originally given the bell to the church, throwing her jewellery into the bell-metal when it was being cast as an expression of her piety.

It would be impossible to imagine sacrilege of any description happening today for the Minchinhampton church fabric shows every sign of being cared-for, and when I was there in the autumn of 1963 the verger was busy with an electric floor-polisher adding a deeper shine to the waxed floor boards. I doubt if he would have tolerated a speck of dust or a tarnished surface in the whole building. In 1962 the interior was cleaned and re-decorated at the cost of nearly £2,000, the slender bars of the lining of the roof painted delicately with gold and pure clear colours, and making the intricate bosses shine with gold leaf like miniature suns.

The newly whitened walls of the nave make splendid foils for the stained glass windows, the work of the late Herbert Bryans, a pupil of the famous Kempe. On the north side is the Beale Memorial window by Edward Payne, a local craftsman, and here again the colours and drawings are delicate yet strong, reassuring evidence that the insipid prettiness and outworn symbolism of the Victorian period has at last been abandoned and the art come alive again. It is fitting, also, that small pictures of local buildings have been embodied in the design.

Reburnished and shining bright the church has shed the grey melancholy and the smell of the mouldering past which permeates so many old churches. To your hardened romantic this may mean the loss of its charm but I prefer the smell of floor polish and light flooding through the windows.

Minchinhampton Common has never been cultivated, and whether this is the reason or not it is one of the few places I know on the Cotswolds where a sense of timelessness such as pervades primeval solitudes can sometimes be felt. It has been late evening when this has happened to me, when the horizons have faded into the night sky and the vast plateau stretching far into the distance on every side has reduced human endeavour of the last two thousand years to vanity.

But since reading Mrs. Clifford's theory about the Minchinhampton earthworks in her book on Bagendon the Common has become historically alive for me. Her theory, that the earthworks formed a complex with those of Rodborough and Amberley and may have been the work of Caratacus, son of Cunobelinus, does not seem so startling when one reads the supporting archaeological and topographical information and the fascinating build-up of the evidence.

Until a few years ago the emphasis had been on the Romans because of the literary and archaeological evidence available to the historian, while reliable information about the native tribes who defied the Romans has been tantalizingly vague. We do know that Cunobelinus had two sons, and when he died Togodumnus ruled that part of the kingdom south of the Thames while Caratacus took the country north of it. The brothers attacked Plautius and his invading army independently and both were defeated. Togodumnus died and Caratacus vanished. Four years later he reappeared in Wales leading the resistance of the Silures.

What happened to him and where did he live in the four years from A.D. 43 to 47, between his defeat by Plautius and his emergence as leader of the Silures? Mrs. Clifford suggests that he spent them in the Cotswolds and that his base was the Minchinhampton complex.

Including the earthworks at Rodborough and Amberley this covers some 600 acres and could have held a great number of defenders as well as camp-followers, their horses, cattle and equipment. Mrs. Clifford also includes the Cooper's Hill complex in the north, and the Pinbury Park, Juniper Hill and Water Lane ramparts and ditches in the east, and this can be understood if one considers their position on the triangular-shaped plateau on which they stand. This plateau is some 600 feet high, and it is only on the south-east that earthworks are necessary to defend it; on the other sides a steep escarpment makes a natural defence. The Water Lane earthworks with its remarkably deep rock-cut ditch would form a barrier to progress westward, while the one at Juniper Hill, excavated by Mrs. Clifford, revealed a rampart with a dry-stone wall revetment. With the single line of earthwork in Pinbury

Park, known as the Nun's Walk, they would have formed a considerable obstacle to enemies on the westward route.

The recent Bagendon excavations have shown that the Cotswolds were occupied by the Belgic Dobunni under Catuvellaunian suzerainty; Caratacus as overlord of the Belgic Dobunni would have known the terrain. The surrender to the Romans of the Dobunni who had their capital at Bagendon meant that Caratacus would have to defend himself from the east. Only on the south could he have been outflanked, but in southern Gloucestershire and Somerset the Dobunni were ruled by Corio who still resisted the Romans and would, therefore, be his allies.

In many ways the Minchinhampton complex fits the need of Caratacus for a base for gathering followers and equipment to enable him to continue the struggle against Rome. He was certainly not the only British king to hide in a difficult terrain while gathering forces to make a new attack.

The theory that Caratacus would want to appear to the Silures not as a vanquished ruler but as an ally and potential leader with a strong supporting army is a likely one and to achieve this meant spending some years in preparation. In the Cotswolds he could live off the country and by raids and quick retirement behind the defences of the rock-cut ditch and stone ramparts of his encampment harass those who had submitted to Roman rule. Iron for weapons and tools could be obtained from the Forest of Dean nearby.

When the time came, as Collingwood put it, "to cut himself loose from his own country and rouse in the tribes as yet untouched by Rome a spirit of resistance to the invaders" Minchinhampton made a good point of departure. The river gravels of the Frome stretch down to the Severn, and this would make travelling with an army easier, as well as being the shortest route to the loop of the Severn where it is joined by the Frome. A crossing of the Severn is possible at this point. It has been demonstrated that at suitable tides it is even possible to wade across it.

We know Caratacus reached Wales and that when in A.D. 47 Ostorius Scapula succeeded Plautius he found hostile "raiders" harassing Roman "allies". Tacitus says that the leader of these raiders was Caratacus.

This is only a simplified outline of Mrs. Clifford's exciting and gallant attempt to explain the linear earthworks on the Minchin-hampton and neighbouring commons. Whether or not it will stand the test of time or become one of the many theories to be superseded by new findings later on remains to be seen, but the boldness of the conception must always stir the imagination. And that is what the layman, at least, hopes the archaeologist will do.

XVII

ALONG THE WESTERN EDGE

From Bath a road north of the Avon on the site of an ancient trackway climbs past tumuli and earthworks to pass over Lansdown where Sir Bevil Grenville led his cavaliers against the Roundheads in July 1643 and died at the point of victory. On a brilliantly lit day when shafts of sunlight and racing cloud shadows play over the prospect the view from Lansdown can be breathtaking, and I have often wondered if any of the men engaged in that battle catching a glimpse of it felt a pang of anguish for the beauty of a world they might be seeing for the last time.

Undulating but keeping high the road goes on over Freezing Hill to Tog Hill, another famous Cotswold borderland viewpoint, where one sees below a patchwork pastoral of fields and woods and to the west beyond a dark haze that is the smoke of Bristol. The old road meets the A46 at Oldfield Gate, to continue as the main road past the eastern edge of Dyrham Park. This is the Dyrham of the *Anglo-Saxon Chronicle* where the battle was fought in A.D. 577 which decided the fate of Roman Cirencester, Gloucester and Bath.

We have two possible derivations of the name Dyrham, DEOR-HAMM, from the Anglo-Saxon meaning a deer enclosure, in which case it is the earliest recorded deer park in the country, and the other from the British DWR, or water, because of the many springs coming out of the surrounding hill-slopes forming the River Boyd. It was these springs and the Boyd that were used to provide water for the canal, cascades and numerous fountains of the Dutch gardens of Dyrham Park in the early eighteenth century.

Camden first recorded the local tradition giving Dyrham as the site of the famous battle, and the earthworks and terraces on Hinton Hill high above the village have long been thought the site, though the more cautious historians of today describe it less decisively as being "the remains of a Saxon settlement"; this

statement will probably be clarified when and if the earthworks are excavated.

I suppose it depends upon the time and season and one's mood, but on the autumn evening I visited it everything combined to evoke a feeling that the place was pregnant with antiquity, the orange sunset with windblown tatters of grey cloud across it, the loneliness, and the clear view of the high ridge on the skyline, a ridge holding the trackway going over Freezing Hill and leading to a crossing of the Avon near Bath available for marching or fleeing warriors. It was easy to let my imagination play on the significance of a victory which enabled the Saxons to reach the Bristol Channel and cut off the Welsh Britons from their friends and allies in the south-west and the few remaining in southern and central Britain.

The earthwork is cut through by the B4465 from Tolldown to Pucklechurch and the making of this road may have obliterated the original entrance to the camp. On the right from Tolldown, just below the crest of the hill, the bank is covered with a narrow belt of rough woodland and the earthwork difficult to see plainly because of the many small depressions, the remains of old quarryings, obscuring its vicinity. Across the road behind a tall hedge, however, a wide green bluff bears a curving rampart some eight feet high on the inner edge and much higher on the outer, a defence from the open plateau which gradually decreases as the hilltop slopes away in a steepish, terraced fall. This wide terrace encircles part of the earthwork, and other terraces are stepped on the sides of a coombe where the headland curves like an arc to enfold them. The bright green of cultivated grass inside the rampart makes a vivid contrast with the grey-green of old turf on the banks and terraces. On the banks are worn patches revealing limestone brash and small isolated rocks.

On the other side of the terraced coombe the long dry-stone wall enclosing Dyrham Park can be seen, the park land bordering the wall still keeping a woldish character. A few trees and clumps of trees are isolated in the wide green acres. When I saw it cattle browsed there, but a herd of deer would have made the picture complete.

The big house, the church and the village lie well below the hill-top, reached from the Pucklechurch road by small winding

Almshouses at Wotton under Edge

lanes so that they seem hidden away in the heart of the hills. Lengths of lichened walls of stone give the area a distinct Cotswold character, though only a few of the houses are in the true vernacular and the big house not at all. The main part was designed by Talman in 1698 for William Blaythwayt, who was Secretary of State to William III. Sacheverell Sitwell describes it as a smaller compact Chatsworth with an orangery.

Contemporary writers say that as Comptroller of Works Talman behaved spitefully to Christopher Wren during the building of Hampton Court, regarding him as a serious rival, and it is one of time's little ironies that Talman, who designed Chatsworth and four great halls in the City of London, the Fishmongers', Haberdashers', Drapers' and Taylors', is little known today though everyone has heard of Christopher Wren, at least as the designer of St. Paul's.

The mansion of Dyrham Park with its imposing frontage, like all symbols of wealth and power that have outlived their purpose, looks a little desolate today, though its stone, from a Tolldown quarry a mile or so away, has mellowed beautifully and it is well-tended by the National Trust. It has not been left as an empty shell but contains a living centre, part of it being divided into flats. The National Trust booklet gives a history of the house and the families who once lived there. Memorials of these families are to be found in the church, perched on a narrow shelf close by the house, and it is from the tiny churchyard one can look over a high stone wall which seems to be keeping the church and its churchyard from slipping down into the park and get a good view of the west front with its flattened scrolls supporting the balcony and the lead figure of Hermes poised as if about to take off into the sky.

The fabric of the church is now mostly Perpendicular, with a south porch whose quatrefoiled parapet gives it a special grace. A brass with a double canopy commemorates Maurice Russel who died in 1401 and his wife Isobel, the effigy of Sir Maurice being in armour with a lion at his feet. There is also the tomb of George Wynter (died 1581) with his wife and their eleven children, while a tablet on the south wall is to John and to Francis Wynter whose daughter Mary married Sir William Blaythwayt in 1686, but who died before the present house was built.

The elaborate frontages of the mansion are but simple designs compared with the formal patterns of the gardens as shown in Kip's View published in Sir Robert Atkyns' history of Gloucestershire in 1712. One would be tempted to believe the artist had been driven to excess by his enthusiasm if Bigland did not confirm his picture. "Every caprice of Dutch style which could be affected by Art abounded at Dyrham, where such ornaments were so numerous as to defy both experience and Imitation," he wrote. By 1779 Rudder notes that the park and waterworks are "much neglected and going to decay", and by the end of the eighteenth century the pleasure grounds were "reconciled to the modern taste" as a contemporary put it, and a more natural parkland took their place.

Two miles or so north of Dyrham the A46 passes the eastern fringe of another great park holding Dodington House, designed by James Wyatt, the most popular architect as the eighteenth century came to an end and Adam lost the patronage of the important families. Wyatt was as happily employed designing a gothic Fonthill as classical Dodington with its vast Corinthian portico. The circular lodges, stables and dairies and a private chapel in the form of a Greek cross which he built for Christopher Codrington, the wealthy West Indian landowner who was his patron, show what Sacheverell Sitwell calls "the English genius for Park buildings". The cost was enormous and Wyatt supervised everything down to the smallest detail of the furnishings.

The chapel is now the parish church of St. Mary and with the aid of time, weather and use has been absorbed into the English scene, so that it is the stranger who is surprised at finding a parish church in a Cotswold village built in early Renaissance manner.

I once visited the house with a party of elderly countrywomen. Afterwards when we were having tea together and resting our tired feet I tried to discover my companions' reactions to Dodington House. All except one, who preferred Swanage for their annual outing and suspected the organisers of trying to thrust culture upon her, agreed it was a handsome place, but that was all they would say, though a motherly little woman observed that next year she was going to vote for Bristol Zoo as being more homely. By the laughter it provoked I felt this innocent remark contributed as much to the success of the afternoon as James

Wyatt. In the coach going home I sat by the oldest member of the party, who was proud to tell me she had been born and bred on a Cotswold farm. A little flushed by fatigue and excitement she admitted shyly that she felt as if she had been visiting foreign parts. "Like London, or abroad," she said.

The main road follows the line of the ancient trackway to about a mile east of Little Sodbury and then goes north, but the line of the old track can still be followed by a series of footpaths, tracks and lanes to Hawkesbury. There are two parts to Hawkesbury, Hawkesbury Upton on the Cotswold plateau and the older village some 200 or so feet below over the hill, a place less troubled by through traffic and with a church of Saxon foundation, traces of which can still be seen in the base of the shaft of the north doorway. Hawkesbury Hill has a tower topped with a cross erected in memory of General Lord R. E. H. Somerset who died in 1842, and this memorial, as such landmarks will, has made the hill rather than the General, known for miles around.

Continuing due north past the monument for about two and a half miles a minor road turns off at Wortley along Ozleworth Bottom, the largest of those ravine-like valleys characteristic of this part of the Cotswolds. It eats its way into the countryside, flanked by thickly wooded slopes and intersected by twisting paths, a secret hidden place full of enchantment for naturalists and those seeking quiet ways.

Climbing out of the bottom through the grounds of Ozleworth Park one comes unexpectedly to a mansion, a farm and a tiny church. It was a sleepy hazy September afternoon when I went there, the autumnal feeling intensified by an occasional blaze of russet where the limb of an old beech had succumbed early to the season's decay. Wine-red berries on old thorns, chestnut foliage turned to tarnished gold, and a fall of yellow leaves gentle as snowflakes made the way to the church a progression into the autumn of the poets. It seemed an intrusion to walk along the drive past the beautifully kept lawns and the magnificent spreading cedars but there was no other way to reach the church tucked behind the house in a farmyard. It was no ordinary farmyard, however, for a handsome Italianate gateway led out of it into the farm proper, giving a charming vista of fields and a wooded coombe beyond through the tall arch.

The little Norman church of St. Nicholas has a hexagonal tower, the windows on each side of the top stage having two round-headed lights divided by a pillar decorated with a single line of cable moulding. In the interior the arch opening into the nave has boldly-cut chevron carving, rare on Cotswold, and the south doorway has carved capitals of a later Norman date. Its remote position and miniature size, the indefinable atmosphere of a forgotten past gives it a special place amongst the churches of Cotswold.

The drive winds upward to pass a small group of cottages at the Lodge gates, and then a narrow twisting road overhung by trees brings one to the high country above Wotton and finally out to the main road, passing on the left the drive to Newark Park, now in the care of the National Trust, whose battlemented mansion is said to have been built out of the remains of Kingswood Abbey by Sir Nicholas Pointz. In Kingswood itself the fifteenth-century gateway is all that is left of the abbey.

Kingswood, about a mile south-west of Wotton, has become a small manufacturing centre and has the look of a village half in and half out of the countryside. It has a few pleasant cottages near the abbey gateway, some rather drab council houses just off the main road, and one modern building of note, a grammar school opened at the end of 1962. It stands rather bleakly in a field, but given a setting of lawns and a few trees I can imagine the cubes and oblongs of its design settling into place. Though the architect has completely rejected the Cotswold vernacular it bears the name of an ancient foundation, Katherine, Lady Berkeley's Grammar School. The original school founded in 1384 by Dame Katherine Berkeley was the first free grammar school in England. Richard II gave her the license "considering that the desire of many who wish to learn grammar, which is the foundation of all other literal arts, is often frustrated through poverty". I feel Dame Katherine, being a forward-looking woman, would have approved of the new building.

`As well as the Ozleworth Bottom there is another smaller deeply-incised valley, Tyley Bottom, inaccessible except on foot, with wooded steeps shutting in its tiny stream and footpaths climbing upward to reach a labyrinth of gated tracks leading to Bagpath and Newington Bagpath's tiny church on a knoll beside a castle mound. From the higher fields one looks down on wooded ravines and small coombes fretting the scene and it is hard to believe it is only a mile or so as the crow flies to the busy A4135. Its seclusion is accentuated by the way one must climb up and down the winding precipitous narrow roads to get in or out of it, a nightmare to the learner driver but enchanting to the naturalist because of its wayside plants and bird life. The people who lived in the cottages clinging to the hillsides or in the narrow bottoms must have been isolated in times of bad weather before the days of the Land Rover. Yet Newington Bagpath had a colony of weavers, and the valley of the infant Avon its mills in the eighteenth century. Prehistoric man and the Romans knew it also, for there are tumuli and a long barrow on the plateau above the valley and the site of a Roman settlement not far from the main road.

Wotton under Edge has its own historian in Mr. E. S. Lindley. In his book *Wotton under Edge* published by the Museum Press in 1962 can be found a detailed account of its life from the first record in a Saxon Royal Charter of A.D. 940, when King Edmund of Wessex leases to thegn Edric four hides of land in "Wudetun", to our own day. Mr. Lindley has gathered his material from every available document and source and his book shows plainly how the past has shaped the town of today, street by street and building by building.

I have always found Wotton a fascinating place, and this must be the excuse for putting down my own impressions, recommending those who would learn more about its history to read Mr. Lindley's scholarly book.

The town is not particularly Cotswold in appearance, though the Cotswold influence is apparent, for it was once occupied with the wool and clothing trades, especially the latter. It possesses a character unlike any other Cotswold town, partly because of its position half in and half out of the valley with the bluffs and knolls topped with earth-works and tumuli sheltering it from the harsher winds of the plateau, and partly because it has not yet been overtaken by the modern blight which nowadays makes all places look the same. Its early history is intricately woven into that of the great Berkeley family but the domination is not obvious.

In bad times, as when the bottom dropped out of the clothing trade, there was considerable makeshift, and evidence of this still survives in odd corners of down-at-heel picturesquesness such as mill buildings turned into tenements and then, as times became more prosperous, into flats and dwellings. There is a medley of building styles and materials but, what at first surprises in a district where there is much woodland, no half-timbered houses of any note, but this can be accounted for by a disastrous fire which swept the town in the seventeenth century. A few pleasant eighteenth-century houses, rows of cottages perched on narrow terraces showing a crazy jumble of roof angles and colours, tall narrow houses slipped in between larger ones like afterthoughts, mills and warehouses of small dark red brick, gaunt, a little decayed and patched in haphazard fashion, and a main street that climbs steeply up a hill lined with shops and dwellings of various sizes and shapes, including a few with the gables and mullions of Cotswold tradition. In Wotton, however, they paint the drip mouldings and often cover the stone walls with a kind of pebble-dash or stucco.

At the top of the High Street as though keeping an official but amiable eye on the town stands the police station, with its name in large stone letters above the door. It is a square, flat-fronted house, its front windows curtained daintily and showing vases of flowers, thus suggesting that a visit there would be something of a social occasion with tea in the parlour, perhaps, and pleasant conversation. I must admit, though, that this is only the impression given by the front; there is a more work-a-day department round the corner in a side street.

The shops are small enough to be individual, efficient and pleasantly human; no Woolworth's or other great impersonal store spoils the façade.

One is reminded that Wotton is on the edge of Cotswold country in Church Street, where the almshouses given by Hugh Perry in 1638 have six steep gables in a row and two mullioned windows beneath each of them with an archway in the middle, built in the true Cotswold style. Hugh Perry was an alderman of London, but he was born in the town and so remembered it in his charities. He must also have been a wool merchant for there is a carving of a woolsack over the archway above the square tablet recording the foundation.

The front has been recently cleaned and renovated and the creamy-buff of the oolite stands out as if fresh from the quarry, but as always, Wotton has its own way with the stone, for the mouldings over the archway are accentuated by a thin line of black paint with the woolsack completely black and the simple curved ornamentation over it also picked out in this way. It has been done so neatly that even the purist who detests painted stone must confess it a pleasant adornment. There is a delightful vista through the archway into the courtyard with a centre rose-plot, and when I saw it last summer roses made a glow of bright colour for the occupants whose tiny dwellings are set round three sides of the courtyard. The fourth side is partly filled by a small, homely, whitewashed chapel with a mossy Cotswold stone roof.

The parish church has suffered several severe restorations and the stone of its tower ornamented with ball flowers in the two lower stages is marred by a dark scale eating into the surface of the stone. This is a blemish which afflicts other buildings in the town and may be the reason why the stone is sometimes painted or covered with pebbledash. The church contains one of the most beautiful memorial brasses in the county. On a Purbeck marble tomb lies the full-size effigy of Thomas, fifth Baron Berkeley (died 1417), shown in close-fitting armour with a finely chased gorget decorated with four tiny mermaids, his feet resting on a very appealing-looking lion, while his wife, Margaret, who lies beside him wears a simple flowing gown and has a small dog at her feet.

The organ was originally in St. Martin-in-the-Fields, where it is said Handel played on it. It came to Wotton in 1800, and is still in its original mahogany case. From three rounded bosses, their mouldings beautifully turned, fall swags of flowers, fir cones and tassels, while below them a squared panelling gives it dignity and the good proportions the period excelled in.

My small boy acquaintance, Richard, shares my pleasure in visiting Wotton, but not for the same reasons. I had taken him with me on one of my journeys across the wolds, and our picnic lunch of Cornish pasties had disappointed him. As a compensation I promised we would stop at Wotton to buy sweets and a small toy. When we arrived it was early-closing day. We wandered around looking for at least one shop in a back street which might be open and came upon a bubble-gum machine displaying its wares in a round glass globe outside a closed shop. His eyes lit up with delight, a fiendish delight it seemed to me, for we both knew this extraordinary substance was forbidden him, and having let him down badly over the early closing I was obviously powerless to assert my authority. I succumbed, of course. There were still a couple of hours before we could reach home and I had several calls to make which Richard, who never suffered in silence, could turn into near disasters. It was worth it, I felt afterwards, not only because the bubble gum wrapped him in a blissful content but because I could add another of those little songs he invents to keep his elders in their place to my collection. At intervals when he tired of making strange plopping noises as the revolting rubber bubbles broke from his lips he sang one of his little chants quietly to himself.

> Mummy says bubble gummy
> is narsty,
> But Ricky likes it better than
> Cornish parsty.

Climbing north out of Wotton past the old quarries the B4058 meets the main Dursley-Cam road in a couple of miles and soon after a precipitious winding road leads down to Uley, Owlpen and the maze of little roads under the edge. Unlike the plateau the fields are smaller and of many shapes, enclosed with hedges instead of stone walls, and one hears the sound of trickling water in the ditches while robins and blackbirds haunt the thickets. The best overall pictures of the little industrial towns are obtained from the top of the edge where distance and the wide landscape gives them a pleasant pictorial quality not so evident on closer acquaintance, though their sprawl of new houses and factories working full-time is a pleasanter sight than the deserted mills and crumbling cottages of the bad times of the early nineteenth century. Dursley and Cam are prosperous today providing employment for miles around.

From these winding roads under the edge, as far as Frocester and beyond the top and upper flanks of a long-backed isolated hill can be seen above the hedge-tops and from gaps made by field gates. Long before I knew its name it teased my imagination, whether I saw it from the top of the scarp rising out of the Vale or glimpsed its bulk from below. Its name is Cam Long Down and I soon discovered it had a folk tale woven about it, one of those tales whose origin goes far back in time. The same story, with local variants, of course, is told about the Wrekin in Shropshire and Cley Hill in Wiltshire, both being hills dominating the surrounding countryside.

Lewis Wiltshire tells the story in his *Vale of Berkeley*, and it concerns the devil who, having a grudge against Gloucestershire because of its many religious houses, decided to dam the Severn and drown the people of Gloucester. He went up to the hills above Dursley with a gigantic wheelbarrow and spade, and filled the wheelbarrow with a large chunk of Cotswold and pushed it down into the Vale. It was a hot day and the load was heavy. The devil sat down to rest. Along comes a cobbler from the opposite direction who had been collecting shoes to mend and who carried a string of them round his neck. When the devil asked him how far it was to the Severn the cobbler, no doubt smelling brimstone, grew suspicious. Suspecting the devil's intention he showed him the shoes he was carrying and explained he had already worn them out on the way from the river. Whereupon the devil became discouraged, tipped out his load and made off. The load he tipped out of his giant wheelbarrow became Cam Long Down.

The villages and hamlets under the edge belong more to the edge than the hills though here and there a group of stone cottages, a roof of mossy stone slates or a gothic doorway make one realize one has only to look up and see the wall of the escarpment where the hills begin.

At Frocester, below Stroud, there is one of the largest stone tithe barns in the county, with an immense span of Cotswold tiled roof broken only by a tiny dormer window. It was erected between 1284 and 1306 for Abbot de Gamage, and once served for the collection of the tithes of the Benedictine monastery. The barn measures 184 feet long, thirty feet wide and thirty-six feet high to the roof ridge, the walls to the eaves being twelve feet high, which gives an indication of the steepness of the roof. Inside there are twelve bays, divided by principals fourteen to sixteen feet apart, and these huge principal beams built into the walls, with the aid of massive buttresses outside, support the enormous weight of the stone tiles. Two great cart porches can take loaded

wagons with room to spare, and when I looked inside, sniffing
the familiar dusty smell of straw and corn mingled with the less
pleasant smell of tractor oil, the men unloading a large wagon
looked dwarfed in that shadowy interior.

I think one could claim that barn for Cotswold, not only
because the stone for walls and roof came from the quarries on the
hills but because the abbot owned many a fine manor there and
stored wool from Cotswold sheep as well as corn grown on the
vast fields of the plateau in his barn. Its size makes one wonder if his
tithes were greater than the tenths they were supposed to represent;
otherwise the extent of his territory must have stretched for more
miles than seems possible.

The barn is still in a good condition and has been well-cared for.
Age has settled it more firmly on the ground, darkened the slates
with each season's encrustment of lichen, coloured the walls a
sombre grey and toughened the massive oak beams to an adaman-
tine hardness, but the 650 years of its life have not eaten too dan-
gerously into its substance and it stands as solid and satisfying
today as when the abbot built it. Yoked oxen pulling creaking
carts were probably the first beasts to turn into its porches, and
then the great cart horses with their jingling harness stamping
upon the dusty floor and blowing the dust from their nostrils.
Now the tractor provides the driving power, and loading gear
and elevators raise the bales instead of straining muscles, but the
old barn can still make the Middle Ages seem like yesterday,
absorbing all changes within its vast nave and aisles, for whatever
the method used seed time and harvest must come to the same
conclusion.

Close by the farm is Frocester Court, rebuilt by Sir George
Huntley in 1554 on the site of an establishment belonging to
Gloucester Abbey. One can glimpse its gables and mullioned
windows through the archway of the Tudor Gate House, which
has a half-timbered storey over its entrance. The builder has done
more with the timbers than use them as a framework; they have
been skillfully cut to make a pattern of circles divided by straight
baulks in the centre, the builder fitting in short curved pieces to
make half-circles at the sides and devising the corners to carry on
his design so that all fits neatly into place.

BOOK LIST

Sir Robert Atkyns *Ancient and Present State of Gloucestershire*, 1712
Samuel Rudder *A New History of Gloucestershire*, 1779
Arthur Gibbs *A Cotswold Village*
J. Charles Cox *Gloucestershire*
R. G. Collingwood *Roman Britain*
Percy C. Rushen *History and Antiquities of Chipping Campden*
E. A. B. Barnard *Stanton and Snowshill*
K. G. Ponting *The Wool Trade*, Journal of Textile Institute, XLIV
H. W. Timperley *A Cotswold Book*
Lewis Wiltshire *The Vale of Berkeley*
Edith Brill *The Cotswolds*
Freda Derrick *Cotswold Stone*
Christopher Whitfield *History of Chipping Campden*
H. P. R. Finberg *Gloucestershire*
H. P. R. Finberg (Editor) *Gloucestershire Studies*
Sir John Clark (Editor) *The Campden Wonder*
Elsie M. Clifford *Bagendon: a Belgic Oppidum*
V. H. H. Green *The Young Mr. Wesley*
E. S. Lindley *Wotton under Edge*

INDEX